THE

ARROGANT

AUTOCRAT

The Betrayal of Canada

A New and Better Canada

At Twilight in the Country

Pay the Rent or Feed the Kids

The Vanishing Country

Rushing to Armageddon

The Truth About Canada

THE ARROGANT AUTOCRAT

STEPHEN HARPER'S TAKEOVER OF CANADA

MEL HURTIG

MHP
MEL HURTIG PUBLISHING
Vancouver

Mel Hurtig Publishing
Vancouver

Cataloguing data available from Library and Archives Canada
ISBN 978-0-9940901-0-2 (paperback)
ISBN 978-0-9940901-1-9 (ebook)

15 16 17 18 19   5 4 3 2 1

"A few more years of Stephen Harper and we're going to have to change the name of our country."

PETER C. NEWMAN

"I think we're regressing... I think we're regressing in terms of the context of our place in the world. It drives me crazy. There was a time in Canada twenty or thirty years ago when we had a powerful voice as a broker in international issues. We were effective around the world. We were highly regarded. That has deteriorated significantly and I feel we're losing—the world is losing—a tremendous opportunity to have a nation whose voice was once a clarion call and is now largely disregarded. So... whether it's our absence on climate change or our freezing of foreign aid and our inability to deal with some of the global health issues, Canada has pulled back from influence and that frankly unsettles me because the world needs voices of principle and we are no longer a voice of principle."

STEPHEN LEWIS, former Canadian Ambassador
to the United Nations and UN Special Envoy on HIV/AIDS
(from CBC's *The Current*, 10th Anniversary Show).

Dedicated to my four wonderful grandsons:

Max, Ben, Elliot & Sacha

CONTENTS

ACKNOWLEDGEMENTS

WITH SPECIAL THANKS to: Jillian Skeet, Jan Walter, David Macdonald, Peter C. Newman, Lawrence Martin, Stephen Lewis, David Suzuki, Maude Barlow, Seth Klein, Armine Yalnizyan, The Canadian Centre for Policy Alternatives, Sherri Torjman, Carol Goar, Mark Jaccard, Jim Stanford, Jeffrey Simpson, Rick Smith, Hugh Segal, Campaign 2000, Art Eggleton, Ed Finn, Janine Brodie, Douglas Gibson, Marci McDonald, Anita Nickerson, Fair Vote Canada, Dean Beeby, The Pembina Institute, Alex Himelfarb, Michael Burton, Susan Minsos, Jessie Finkelstein, Ed Broadbent, Elizabeth May, Errol Mendes, Nathan Cullen, Donald Savoie, Tom Flanagan, Thomas Walkom, Laurel Rothman, Trish Hennessy, Peter Julian, Henri Sader, Jean-Pierre Kingsley, Erin Weir, Laurel Rothman, Bruce Campbell and Ken Battle.

— INTRODUCTION —

STEPHEN HARPER'S TAKEOVER OF CANADA

I HAVE SPENT MUCH of my career warning Canadians about the increasing threat that foreign corporate take-overs of our companies and resource sectors pose to our sovereignty and to the overall economic and social well-being of our country.

Through decades of sounding the alarm on takeovers, in book after book, and in hundreds of speaking engagements across the country, I never imagined that the greatest threat would come from the takeover of our democratic institutions by one politician determined to remake our nation according to his own values and priorities.

That one politician is, of course, Stephen Harper.

Stephen Harper has been able to take advantage of a dysfunctional electoral system to seize majority power in Parliament with only 39.6 percent of the votes cast by Canadians. Majority power has allowed him to systemically dismantle our democracy, crippling or eliminating many of the institutions that have been developed over decades to deliver programs to Canadians and to allow for a democratic exchange of information and ideas between the electorate and the elected.

I have written and published many books about Canada, many of them bestsellers, but this short book is unquestionably the most important because it is about the most serious takeover that has ever occurred in Canada, the takeover of our democracy.

They say that voters' memories are short. When I began going through the material I had compiled on the actions of the Harper government over the last few years, I was stunned by how many past events had slipped from present memory, and stunned again by the scope of the damage he has done to our democracy, our reputation and to so many important Canadian institutions.

Numerous books have been written in recent years about Stephen Harper, his policies, and his governing style. Many provide detailed in-depth accounts of the inner workings of government, while others focus on particular issues. This book does not attempt to replicate their work.

My purpose is to provide a succinct overview and reminder of the scope of the damage Stephen Harper has done to our country, and to soundly refute the claims repeatedly made by his government that they have been wonderful economic managers since they took power. The evidence is overwhelmingly to the contrary as you will see in the coming pages.

This book is intended as a wake-up call to Canadians to reclaim our democracy and our country before it is too late.

— 1 —
A BROKEN
DEMOCRATIC SYSTEM

H OW COULD THIS possibly have happened?
Or, to be more specific, how could it happen that
a widely-admired, progressive country like Canada, a country regarded around the world as a remarkably fortunate, highly desirable destination for prospective immigrants from every continent, finds itself in its present predicament?

How did we end up with a far right, ultra-conservative prime minister who has launched an all-out assault on our democracy and who is—as quickly as possible—dismantling many institutions that Canadians hold dear?

What kind of democracy do we have when the government suppresses and tightly controls information that is essential to good governance, violates long-held democratic principles, and undermines so many of the processes that support democracy?

Our elected members of parliament and even our cabinet ministers are restricted by the Prime Minister's Office in who they can talk to, when they can give a speech, what press interviews they can accept, and the nature of their comments to the press and the public.

Brent Rathgeber, a former Tory backbencher and now independent member of parliament for Edmonton-St. Albert, provides a rare glimpse inside the tightly controlled Conservative caucus in his book, *Irresponsible Government: The Decline of Parliamentary Democracy in Canada*. He describes how, under Harper, MPs have been "reduced to cheer-leading and barking on command." He says Conservative backbenchers are permitted to say very little in the House of Commons and are punished if they step out of line. The Conservative caucus, "is more of a pep rally and doesn't include votes on policy in advance." And, "there is very little to hold the government to account."[1] In a March 29, 2013 editorial, the *Toronto Star* observed that the Prime Minister's Office "is plumbing new depths in expecting the government caucus to perform like trained seals that clap their flippers and bark in unison ... Harper has proven to be a notorious control freak."[2]

Canadian journalist Lawrence Martin has written frequently about Harper's authoritarian methods. His book, *Harperland*, is subtitled: *The Politics of Control*. It could equally have been *The Control of Politics*, because that is what Harper has achieved with remarkably little opposition from the Canadian media. Martin writes of Harper's "ironclad, dictatorial control of communications," and what some have described as a "Genghis Khan" style of politics.[3]

In early 2011, it was reported that Harper's team was even attempting to rebrand the government of Canada as the

"Harper Government." Despite denials, several public servants told the *Canadian Press* they had received instructions directly from *"the Centre*—meaning the Prime Minister's Office and the Privy Council Office that serves the Prime Minister" that *Government of Canada* was to be replaced by *Harper Government.*[4] Liberal MP Dominic LeBlanc commented to CBC News at the time: "It's not Stephen Harper's government, it's the government of all Canadians. You'd expect this kind of directive to be issued by the ministry of information in North Korea."[5]

This tight control on communication and information has extended far beyond caucus members and cabinet ministers to bureaucrats, government scientists, and even to free expression by the public. In Harper's Canada, if citizens want to appear before the National Energy Board about a proposed pipeline, to cite just one of the major issues of concern in the country today, they must first fill in an application requesting the privilege of having their voices heard. The government's new guidelines for the NEB have created rules that act to limit citizens' participation. Under these rules, one must be directly affected by a project—i.e. the proposed pipeline's route will run through your property—to be permitted to speak or to make a submission to the Board. If you are not considered a "stakeholder," then your views as a citizen are not welcome.[6]

The list of directors of Canadian agencies and institutions who have been fired or resigned in protest as a result of clashes with the Harper government continues to grow. Linda Keen was fired from her role as Nuclear Safety Commissioner after she shut down a nuclear reactor, citing safety concerns. Adrian Measner was dismissed as the head of the Canadian Wheat Board for opposing the dismantling of that body. Pat Stogan, the first commanding officer of Canadian soldiers in Afghanistan, was terminated as the Veterans' Ombudsman after he criticized the provisions of the new Veterans' Charter. The list goes on.

What happened to former Parliamentary Budget Officer Kevin Page highlights the difficulties that many of Canada's senior bureaucrats and agency leaders have faced under the Harper regime. The Parliamentary Budget Office was created by the Harper Conservatives supposedly to enhance government transparency and hold the government accountable by scrutinizing its expenditures. But when Page began to issue pointed criticisms of government practices, the government bristled. Page was aghast at the introduction of proposed changes to Canada's pension provisions, without benefit of the traditional White Paper to help analyze the policy implications and invite comment.

Such public utterances were met with cuts to the Parliamentary Budget Office's budget.

Page was forced to scramble for the funds he needed to do his job and was consistently blocked by the Prime Minister's Office. Incredibly, he was accused of overstepping his mandate. As NDP Leader Thomas Mulcair told the *Globe and Mail,* anyone who "dares stand up to [the Conservatives], that doesn't tell them exactly what they want to hear, they will be shut down."[7]

Page himself said that he didn't think members of parliament were making informed decisions because they were not getting the information they required.[8]

Time after time after time, government departments failed to respond when the Parliamentary Budget Office requested information. According to *Post Media News*, "The federal government has refused to give the parliament budgetary watchdog copies of the bids that ultimately won nearly $33 billion worth of work for shipyards in Halifax and Vancouver under the government's national shipbuilding strategy."[9] Page wrote to the deputy minister in charge, asking for copies of the relevant bids, but the requests were denied. Unbelievably, the Parliamentary Budget Officer was reduced to filing Access to Information requests for departmental data to which he is statutorily entitled.

Similarly, federal departments have repeatedly denied requests from opposition members of parliament to provide more detailed explanations of spending. According to the *Canadian Press,* in March of 2014, "eleven different federal departments refused to provide Parliament with their plans to address concerns raised by the Auditor General, despite being mandated to do so."[10]

When Harper was in opposition, he strenuously campaigned for easier access to information but he has lost his appetite for it now that he is in government. In 2006 he promised the Federal Information Commissioner the power to order the release of information, but such a promise has proven meaningless. In 2008, the Harper government eliminated the Access to Information Database widely used by journalists, researchers, experts and the public to identify and request documents previously obtained by other users.[11] There have been ever longer delays in fulfilling requests for information from the public, the press or the opposition. And when documents are released, they are frequently blackened out beyond usefulness.

Susan Delacourt, Ottawa reporter for the *Toronto Star,* says that the Harper government is building a stone wall around information. "It's now standard, for instance, for reporters to submit questions in writing to the government only to wait hours, days or even weeks for a committee-approved response."[12] The *Star's* public editor, Kathy English, cites one reporter's request for information about a US-Canada border initiative. The response from the government referred the reporter to the text of Canada's Economic Action Plan, advising that "many of these goals have already been achieved. A list of accomplishments that have been announced can be found at www.borderactionplan.gc.ca." English calls the government's response "a bunch of malarkey," and says, "It shuts the door to real information from the minister in charge and keeps the columnist—but more importantly [the public]—in the dark."[13]

Instead of parliament becoming more accountable, the opposite has been occurring. An international report issued in 2013, by The Centre for Law and Democracy, ranked the Harper government as fifty-fifth in the world for upholding freedom of information principles. This was a drop from 40th in the world in 2011. The request for the government's rebuttal to the report under Access to Information took five months to fulfill! The law requires a response within thirty days.[14] Rather than benefitting from enhanced access to information, Canadians are expected to accept denial of information.

Nor does the Harper government respond to tough or uncomfortable questions. When the termination of Canada Post's door-to-door mail delivery was announced, reporters complained no one—not the minister responsible for Canada Post, Lisa Raitt, nor Canada Post executives—was available to answer the obvious questions. The level of information manipulation and control by the seat of power in Ottawa is unprecedented. Virtually everyone in government must have their messages vetted by the PMO or the Privy Council Office. "Even the most harmless announcements (Parks Canada's release on the mating season of the black bear, for example) require approval from the top,"[15] according to one report.

Communication is controlled through the use of Message Event Proposals (MEP) which must be submitted by cabinet ministers, public servants and members of parliament prior to events or information releases. *Canadian Press* obtained almost 1,000 pages of MEPs through Access to Information and found they covered myriad matters, large and small, from an MP's visit to a seniors' home to "a journalism student's innocuous query about Africa." Those completing MEPs must request authorization to attend an event or release information and, if approval is granted, they are given direction on all aspects of the event or statement, including key messages to be emphasized, the desired sound-bites, appropriate attire, background details, photo shoots, and more.[16]

This is the behaviour of an autocratic, dictatorial regime, practices that even then House of Commons Speaker Peter Milliken felt compelled to challenge. After the Harper government refused to turn over requested information on the details of proposed bills and expenditures to Parliament, Speaker Milliken ruled the government in contempt of parliament, a first in Canadian history.

The government's assault on democracy has taken many forms. Harper has prorogued parliament on three occasions during his tenure—in 2008, 2009, and again in 2013. According to Elizabeth May, leader of the Green Party and a lawyer, the prorogations of 2008 and 2009 constitute an abuse of power seen on only one other occasion, under John A. Macdonald in 1873. May points out that proroguing parliament is a normal practice to end a session of the House, with the expectation that it will open later with a new agenda and a speech from the throne. However, it is an abuse of power when it is used to avoid a vote that would likely bring down the government. May writes:

> "Modern parliamentary democracy rests on a single great principle: The government must have the consent of the governed. This consent is delegated by the people to their MPs. The government must then be able to carry the 'confidence' of the House of Commons. Majority governments rarely lose that confidence, minority governments often do. When the government cannot carry the House, it falls.
>
> "Suspending parliament to dodge a vote the government fears it will lose is so deeply undemocratic, it should never have been [accepted] by politicians, the media or the governor-general."[17]

Stephen Harper has also routinely invoked "time allocation" and closure to stifle and limit debate in the House of Commons, particularly on the massive omnibus bills that have come to characterize his legislative style. An omnibus bill is a bill crammed full of other pieces of legislation that at one time were presented, debated and voted on individually. Harper's first omnibus budget bill targeted environmental regulations, a process that continued with later bills.

Referring to an omnibus bill tabled in October, 2013, the *Toronto Star* reported:

> "The Harper government has once again resorted to sneaking ideology-driven policy in through the back door by cramming the change (to the public service) into Bill C-4, a 321 page 'omnibus' budget bill . . . that contains a slew of unrelated measures. Apart from union rights, the bill affects Supreme Court appointments, employment insurance, workplace safety, veterans' affairs, conflict-of-interest, solicitor-client privileges, immigration policy and more. There is no way MPs can give this bulky tome the study it deserves in the short time available. It's just the latest Conservative affront to Parliament."[18]

Ironically, back in 1994, as a Reform Party MP, Stephen Harper took exception to such bills. *Hansard* of March 25th, 1994 records his words:

> "Mr. Speaker, I would argue that the subject matter of the bill is so diverse that a single vote on the content would put members in conflict with their own principles . . .
>
> "Second, in the interest of democracy I ask: How can members represent their constituents on these various areas when they are forced to vote in a block on such legislation and on such concerns? We can agree with some of the measures but oppose others. How do we express our views

and the views of our constituents when the matters are so diverse? Dividing the bill into several components would allow members to represent views of their constituents on each of the different components in the bill."[19]

The omnibus bill that Harper objected to at the time was Liberal budget Bill C-17, which was 21 pages in length and related solely to spending reportedly affecting 11 statutes. By comparison, Harper's 2010 budget came in at over 800 pages and contained many non-budgetary items. His omnibus legislation has also included Bills C-38 and C-45, each coming in at over 400 pages and containing a shopping list of unrelated Conservative policy hobby horses. Referring to Harper's earlier objections to omnibus legislation, constitutional and human rights lawyer Errol Mendes wrote in the *Globe*:

> "Mr. Harper seems to be implying that omnibus legislation would violate the parliamentary privileges of all MPs. If that is what he was asserting, it would imply that he as prime minister would be intentionally undermining the parliamentary and constitutional democracy of Canada."[20]

Harper subsequently sent various parts of the budget bill to 11 committees for "review and potential amendment." NDP House Leader Nathan Cullen said of the process:

> "Most committees only have a couple of hours to study hundreds of clauses. Witnesses Conservatives do not like are blocked and accountability is being avoided at all costs. It

is now becoming clear that their plan to have committees study these bills was nothing but a sham."[21]

Stephen Harper's disdain for parliamentary committees is now legendary. That attitude was fully on display in a booklet distributed to Conservative caucus members with instructions on "how to unleash chaos while chairing Parliamentary committees." This secret manual, eventually leaked to the media, ran to almost 200 pages and provided committee chairs with suggestions on how to obstruct and delay debate, while directing them to choose witnesses friendly to the Conservative party and the Conservative agenda. According to Lawrence Martin, "if things got really tough and opposition members were on to something that could hurt the government, Conservatives were instructed to end the proceedings by storming out of the committee room."[22]

Thanks to such tactics, Canada's parliament has become a largely ceremonial body, incapable of performing its defining functions of safeguarding public spending and holding ministers to account. Donald Savoie, one of Canada's leading experts on parliamentary democracy says, "between elections prime ministers now operate in the omnipotent manner of kings. Surrounded by subservient cabinet barons, fawning unelected courtiers and answerable to no one, they manage the affairs of state more or less as they please."[23] Indeed, increasingly we've seen our democratic institutions fail to hold those in power to account. As the late Jim Travers, political columnist at the *Toronto Star*, put it, "Once solid institutions are being pulled apart by rising complexity and falling legitimacy... power and control are increasingly concentrated and accountability honoured more in promise than practice."[24]

There has also been a regrettable loss of civility in the conduct of parliamentarians. Contempt for the opposition among many Harper cabinet ministers has been well documented.

This stands in stark contrast to a civilized parliamentary tradition where, political sparring aside, politicians from opposing sides usually exhibit respect for each other outside of chambers and often genuinely like each other.

Former member of parliament and cabinet minister David Emerson, who jumped parties from the Liberals to the Conservatives, couldn't fathom the "intense level of acrimony" among his new Conservative caucus colleagues. With Harper and his circle, it went deep: Emerson spoke of them as "viscerally hating" their political opposition.[25] Liberal MP Keith Martin, who also served in both parties, crossing from the Conservatives to the Liberals, had an experience similar to Emerson's. He described the government side as an environment "that has bred a hatred" towards the Liberal way. He found it particularly strange given the pronounced influence of religion on the party. He understood that Liberals held positions that ran counter to the Conservatives', "but why... hate them?"[26]

Lawrence Martin writes that Harper's attacks on Chrétien and Paul Martin were "over the top." He says, "There is a harshness, a lack of humour, humanity and moderation that disregards the traditions of parliament where all members have a right to be treated as honourable."[27]

Beyond the halls of parliament, the very integrity of our electoral system has come under attack. The robocall scandal made clear that thousands of voters across the country—essentially those who identified themselves as non-Conservatives—were contacted and directed to the wrong polling stations. Is there any more blatant form of corruption in a democracy than the attempt of a governing party to prevent its opposition's supporters from voting?

When the robocall case went to court, the Council of Canadians described the whole legal process as outrageous. The Federal Court confirmed that fraud had taken place but failed to overturn the election results in six affected ridings. Conservative staffer Michael Sona was later found guilty of misleading voters in an effort to prevent them from voting, an indictable offence under the Elections Act. In his decision, the judge stated: "Although the evidence indicates he [Sona] did not likely act alone, he was party to the offence and, as noted previously, there will be a finding of guilt registered."[28]

In light of this scandal, the trustworthiness of Canada's elections—once viewed as among the fairest and most transparent in the world—has been called into question. Thankfully, the fact that the abuse was identified and successfully prosecuted shows that all is not yet completely lost. Despite the burden of a first-past-the-post electoral system that has become dysfunctional in recent years, we have long enjoyed an international reputation as a model democracy with scrupulous measures in place to protect our voting processes. Just as we were once called upon for peacekeeping service in troubled zones, we have often been asked to play a leading role in setting up and overseeing voting mechanisms in new and emerging democracies. Yet thanks to the actions of Conservative operatives, our once admired model has been tainted, raising new questions about the integrity of our entire voting system.

Nor can we forget the Harper government's so-called Fair Elections Act which attempted to disenfranchise large numbers of vulnerable Canadians, citizens who would be unlikely to support the Conservative party at the polls. Under the rules the Conservatives had planned, voters without identification would have no longer been permitted to have someone vouch for them, and they would no longer be permitted to use voter information cards (received in the mail) to prove their address. In 2011, approximately 120,000 voters did not have I.D., while another 400,000 used their voter information card to validate their address. And who are these people? They are primarily students, people who have just moved, members of First Nations living on reserves, seniors and those on low incomes. The new provisions would have undermined the Charter of Rights and the guaranteed right of all Canadians to vote. After Canadians stood in strong opposition to the proposed Act, it was amended to allow a revised form of vouching to take place, but many critics say that many of the other provisions in the Act remain flawed.[29]

Under the Harper government, Canadian civil liberties are also under direct threat. During the G20 Summit in Toronto in June 2010, more than a thousand protesters, including innocent bystanders, were held without charge under abhorrent conditions in what amounted to a shocking violation of civil rights. In his report, Gerry McNeilly, head of the Office of the Independent Police Review Director (Ontario's police watchdog), wrote that there was excessive use of force, rampant violations of the Charter of Rights, unlawful mass arrests and appalling detention conditions that included overcrowding, strip searches, lack of food and water, washroom facilities without privacy and lack of access to lawyers. Many detainees were held for as long as 24 hours.[30]

And now, new anti-terrorism legislation (Bill C-51) aims to legally strip Canadians of more rights and freedoms. Stephen Harper's military enthusiasm has altered the global perception of Canada as a peaceful nation and increasingly placed us on the radar of terrorists. The lone gunman attack on Parliament in the fall of 2014 and new videotaped threats against Canadian targets are Harper's justification for the Anti-terrorism Act. The Harper government wants greater police surveillance powers to monitor Canadians but many fear the bill will be used to stifle legitimate protest and dissent.

The British Columbia Civil Liberties Association has analyzed the anti-terror legislation and warns: "Bill C-51 defines security as not only safeguarding public safety, but also preventing interference with various aspects of public life or "the economic or financial stability of Canada." With this definition, a separatist demonstration in Quebec that fails to get a proper permit, a peaceful logging blockade by First Nations, or environmentalists obstructing a pipeline route could all be seen as threats to national security."[31]

The Act has been described in an Open Letter from 100 Canadian law professors and others as "a dangerous piece of legislation in terms of its potential impacts on the rule of law, on constitutionally and internationally protected rights, and on the health of Canada's democracy."[32]

In a joint statement published in English and French newspapers in February, 2015, four former prime ministers:

Jean Chrétien, Paul Martin, Joe Clark and John Turner, along with five former Supreme Court justices, seven former Liberal solicitor generals and ministers of justice, three past members of the intelligence review committee, two former privacy commissioners and a retired RCMP watchdog, called for stronger oversight of the legislation. The statement said, "Protecting human rights and protecting public safety are complementary objectives, but experience has shown that serious human rights abuses can occur in the name of maintaining national security... Given the secrecy around national security activities, abuses can go undetected and without remedy. This results not only in devastating personal consequences for the individuals, but a profoundly negative impact on Canada's reputation as a rights-respecting nation."[33]

The damage that Stephen Harper has managed to inflict on so many aspects of Canadian democracy in just a few short years is frightening. That we have failed to stop it from happening, even more so. We expect our fellow Canadians—and especially our politicians—to respect the democratic systems, processes and institutions that have been built up over generations. Not only does Stephen Harper demonstrate a lack of respect for the democratic foundations of our nation, all indications are that he is determined to undermine or destroy them. Information is withheld, dissent is stifled, and the checks and balances on government power are eroded or eliminated.

Canadians are quickly losing the ability to have any influence on the decisions made in their name, or any control over the direction in which our country is headed.

— 2 —

HARPER'S WAR
ON THE ENVIRONMENT

WHAT CAN ONE say about Stephen Harper's appalling record on the environment?

Well, for starters, he obviously doesn't care. He doesn't care that climate change is exacting an increasingly heavy human and economic toll on Canada and on the planet. He doesn't care that our country is referred to by many as a "dinosaur" for its regressive stance on the environment, and that we are a frequent recipient of "fossil awards" for pursuing policies that seem designed to ensure human extinction. And he is completely unapologetic and unmoved by the terrible damage he has done to Canada's international reputation.

The days of legitimate debate over whether or not climate change is real are long passed. Yet conservative billionaires like the American Koch brothers are still pouring millions of dollars into the Donors Trust and Donors Capital Funds to support groups that seek to cast doubt on the science behind climate change.[1] As Paul Krugman writes in the *New York*

Times, "Look at the scientists who question the consensus on climate change; look at the organizations pushing fake scandals; look at the think tanks claiming that any effort to limit emissions would cripple the economy. Again and again, you'll find that they're on the receiving end of a pipeline of funding that starts with big energy companies like Exxon Mobil, which has spent tens of millions of dollars promoting climate-change denial, or Koch Industries, which has been sponsoring anti-environmental organizations for two decades."[2]

What these organizations refuse to accept is that we no longer need more science to prove whether or not climate change is real. It has become all too real to those Canadians across the country who have experienced wildfires, floods, ice storms, tornadoes, hurricanes, and temperature extremes unseen in our lifetimes or those of previous generations.

A report from the United Nations' Intergovernmental Panel on Climate Change (IPCC), released at a meeting in Japan in March 2014, stated that "the impacts of global warming are likely to be "severe, pervasive and irreversible." It warned of increased risks of flooding and "impacts on crop yields and water availability."[3] Exaggeration? Fear-mongering? Hardly.

In the summer of 2014, no less than 160 forest fires raged throughout British Columbia, with thousands of people evacuated from their homes.[4] A flash flood along the Thompson River hit Kamloops, turning roads into rivers after a storm dropped 25mm of rainfall in just half an hour.[5] At the same time, the Northwest Territories experienced the worst wildfire season in 30 years, with 130 fires ravaging an area comparable in size to that of Trinidad.[6] Southern

Manitoba and Saskatchewan were in a state of emergency, with extreme flooding destroying crops and damaging homes. The clean-up was expected to take as long as a year.[7]

In June 2014, a state of emergency was declared in the Ontario town of Angus after a tornado touched down leaving unprecedented devastation in its wake and many residents across the province without power.[8] The previous December, Toronto suffered an ice storm followed by record-breaking cold temperatures with a wind-chill that at times fell close to -40°C, paralyzing the region.[9] And, in the summer of 2013, much of the city of Calgary was under water. At last count the clean-up bill was well in excess of $1 billion. It is estimated that a full recovery could take up to a decade.[10] These are but highlights among numerous extreme weather events in Canada over the past two years alone.

One of the lead authors of the IPCC's 2014 report, Dr. Saleemul Huq, was very clear: "Before this we thought we knew [climate change impact] was happening, but now we have overwhelming evidence that this is happening and it is real."[11] Even U.S. Secretary of State John Kerry commented that the cost of inaction on climate change will be "catastrophic." He stated that "unless we act dramatically and quickly, science tells us that our climate and our way of life [are] literally in jeopardy. Denial of the science is malpractice."[12]

So what has been Stephen Harper's response to the warnings from the IPCC and others, and to the abundant evidence of the toll that climate change is taking on our own country?

He has continued to promote the tar sands and pipelines, and use omnibus bills to gut Canada's environmental oversight bodies and regulatory legislation.

The first of these, Bill C-38, was dubbed by some "the Environmental Destruction Act."[13] With Bill C-38, Canada's Environmental Assessment Act was repealed and a new act brought in that waived the need for environmental assessments on projects involving federal money and granted the minister of the Environment wide discretion to decide when and if such assessments would be otherwise required.

The Canadian Environmental Protection Act and the Fisheries Act were weakened, while the Navigable Waters Protection Act was altered so that interprovincial and international pipelines and power lines would be exempt from its provisions.

The National Energy Board was stripped of its decision-making powers for major projects, with reviews limited to two years and the Cabinet given the freedom to ignore Energy Board recommendations. The Species at Risk Act was amended to allow the National Energy Board to issue permits for development without requiring the protection of critical habitats for the projects it approves.

There's still more. Cuts were made to staff and programs in Canada's national parks under the Parks Canada Agency Act. Under the Nuclear Safety Control Act, environmental assessments were moved to the licensing body, the Canadian Nuclear Safety Commission, creating a potential conflict of interest. The National Roundtable on the Environment and the Economy, which brought together industry leaders, environmentalists, First Nations, labour and policy-makers to provide research and to advise the federal government on these two most critical sectors, was axed.

I must mention one more act of the Harper government because of its tragic significance: the Kyoto Protocol

Implementation Act—the legislation that required government accountability, including the reporting of progress on climate change policies—was repealed.[14] We were the first western country to withdraw from the Kyoto Protocol.

In the wake of dire warnings from the IPCC, Stephen Harper continued to press on with the planned tar sands expansion and oil pipeline development. Within two months of the IPCC report's release, the Harper government gave its approval to the controversial Enbridge Northern Gateway pipeline project, an undertaking opposed by large numbers of Canadians including many First Nations along the proposed route.

As reported by Jennifer Ditchburn of the *Canadian Press*, the Northern Gateway decision was made without the customary fanfare, "via a colourless release with the bureaucratic title: *Government of Canada Accepts Recommendation to Impose 209 Conditions on Northern Gateway Proposal*." She wrote, "The usual prefix, *Harper Government*, was absent" from the press release. "The surgical gloves approach speaks volumes on the tough position the Conservative government finds itself in on the project."[15] Not to mention the disingenuous headline, intended to divert attention from the overriding fact of government approval.

A confident leader who believes he is doing his best for the country, with the support of a majority of citizens, would take to the podium with a bevy of ministers and MPs to trumpet this multi-billion dollar enterprise. By contrast, the leader of a so-called democracy who ignores the will of the majority or fears criticism of his actions must resort to slinking in the shadows and to tightly controlling access to himself and to his ministers. Such is Stephen Harper's government.

NDP Leader Thomas Mulcair, remarking on the absence of the prime minister, the minister of the Environment, or any Conservative MP at the time of the news release, accused Conservative MPs from British Columbia—where the pipeline would primarily be located and where the opposition is greatest—as "hiding under their desks."[16]

The attempt to mute the announcement of a decision so important to so many Canadians is not unique. Columnist Jeffrey Simpson of the *Globe and Mail* noted a pattern in the handling of unpopular or controversial information. "When... the news is bad, well, standard procedure is either not to release the information at all, or to post it on a website without telling anyone, hoping the news will pass unnoticed... Such was the case this week when quietly, of course, Environment Canada posted on its website the embarrassing news about the government's expensive and futile measures to combat greenhouse gas emissions... Try as it might, the government could not put lipstick on a pig."[17]

Mark Jaccard is a professor at the School of Resources and Environmental Management at Simon Fraser University, a former Conservative government appointee to the now defunct Roundtable on the Environment and Economy, and a Canadian member of the United Nations' Intergovernmental Panel on Climate Change. He wrote that the Enbridge pipeline would ensure the continuing expansion of tar sands oil production, providing a steady supply of fossil fuels to a planet that needs to go on a strict "low-carb diet." He added, "About 70 percent of global greenhouse emissions come from fossil fuels, production which cannot increase if we are to achieve a major reduction. This means no expansion of coal production, nor of coal ports like the one planned near Vancouver. It means no new investments in the oil sands. And it means no new investments in oil pipelines, like Keystone XL and Northern Gateway."[18]

Scientists around the world, including those of the IPCC, generally agree that global warming that exceeds a two degree Celsius increase from the planetary norm will result in widespread catastrophic impacts. The goal of those supporting Kyoto and other efforts to arrest climate change is to have all countries meet commitments that will ensure we do not exceed that limit.[19] By increasing the extraction of fossil fuels from our soil, Canada will fail to do our part to ensure the world stays below the 2 degree Celsius ceiling. Scientists calculate that Canada's current path could lead to a temperature "increase of six to eight degrees by the year 2100. This kind of increase is predicted to raise sea levels, acidify oceans, cause massive species extinction, and intensify extreme weather events"[20]

University of British Columbia Professor William Rees, who fashioned the concept of the "ecological footprint" has said, "the International Energy Agency and World Bank have recently conceded that even if present agreed-upon policies were implemented, the world is likely headed to four Celsius degrees warming by the end of the century. This would render much of the most heavily populated parts of the earth uninhabitable..."[21]

In early June 2014, U.S. President Barack Obama spoke out strongly and unequivocally. In an interview with Thomas Friedman of the *New York Times*, following proposed new Environmental Protection Agency rules to curb carbon emissions from power plants, Obama said that both the U.S. Department of Defence and the Joint Chiefs of Staff had identified climate change as a major future threat to the U.S. He told Friedman that recent reports had shown that environmental issues were having an impact on both U.S. foreign and domestic policy, citing the example of wildfires that were "consuming a larger and larger portion of the Department of Interior budget ... if we continue to fund fighting fires the same way we've done in the past, all the money for everything else—for conservation, for maintenance of forests—all that money gets used up."[22]

Back in 2009, Canada's then Environment Minister Jim Prentice (now premier of Alberta), indicated in a speech that Canada's policies on the environment would be developed in lock-step with those of the U.S. He stated that Canada and the U.S. would aim for a "cap-and-trade" system and would share targets for cleaner electricity and fuel efficiencies. America, after all, was the country that Stephen Harper told a U.S. think-tank in 1997 was "a light and inspiration for Canadians."[23]

After bowing out of Kyoto, Harper set his own emissions target for 2020 which he confirmed alongside President Obama and other world leaders at the 2009 Copenhagen climate conference. But he failed to follow-up with immediate action to make it achievable. While the U.S. is on course to meet its 2020 target, Canada is not. With the planned tar sands and pipeline expansions, Environment Canada has estimated that we will exceed Harper's emissions limit by as much as 20 percent.[24]

It would appear that in recent months even the U.S. has become too progressive for Stephen Harper. Less than two weeks after President Obama's landmark interview appeared in the *Times*, the Canadian government issued its press release announcing approval of the Enbridge Northern Gateway pipeline.

Harper's handling of the proposed Keystone XL pipeline is no less ham-fisted. In May of 2013, with American opposition to that pipeline on the rise, the Harper government launched a $24 million taxpayer-funded advertising campaign that saw prominent ads placed in U.S. publications and plastered on bus stops and subway stations in Washington, D.C. The theme promoted Canada as a safe and reliable energy supplier. Ironically, surveys later revealed that the main message most Americans took away from the campaign was simply that Canada and the U.S. were friends.[25]

Speaking at a Washington event in opposition to Keystone XL in late 2013, Mark Jaccard told his audience, "On climate, Canada is a rogue state. It's accelerating the global tragedy... The US should reject Keystone XL..."[26]

Even earlier, in 2012, NASA climatologist James Hansen made a presentation to the U.S. Congress in which he argued against Keystone. As he told *Scientific American*, "Moving to tar sands, one of the dirtiest, most carbon-intensive fuels on the planet, is a step in exactly the opposite direction, indicating either that governments don't understand the situation or that they just don't give a damn."[27]

I can't leave this topic without mentioning the dangers posed to Canada's Pacific coast from the proposed Enbridge Northern Gateway pipeline to Prince Rupert and the twinning of the Kinder Morgan pipeline to Burnaby, a suburb of Vancouver. In addition to the climate change arguments and the inherent risks of the pipelines themselves, these projects would result in dramatically increased tanker traffic along British Columbia's pristine coastline. Do we really want over 200 supertankers plying the waters of British Columbia's coastal waters every year, many of them as long as the Empire State Building is high? Some are expected to carry as much as eight times as much oil as the Exxon Valdez, whose spill in Prince William Sound caused an ecological disaster on the Alaskan coastline that remains evident 25 years later.[28]

Opposition to the pipelines in British Columbia runs deep. While early attention focused on the controversial Northern Gateway project, there have been more recent clashes between protesters and Kinder Morgan after the company entered a nature preserve on Burnaby Mountain and began cutting trees to do surveying and testing for the proposed twinning of its existing pipeline.[29] Kinder Morgan, the federal government, the court system and the NEB are all ignoring the will of the City of Burnaby and countless Canadian citizens on this issue. For Finance Minister Joe Oliver to cast such opponents as "foreign-funded", "radical environmental groups," is nothing short of offensive and ignorant.[30]

The potential for catastrophe can't be discounted, nor can the safety record of Kinder Morgan or the possibility of simple human error. In 2007, an excavator ruptured the existing Kinder Morgan pipeline, spewing 1500 barrels of oil into a residential neighbourhood in Burnaby. In March 2006, the BC ferry, Queen of the North, sank after it failed to navigate one of the narrow passages off the coast of Prince Rupert where supertankers would likely sail.

Is there another way? If, as a country, we feel it's absolutely necessary to continue to develop the tar sands (in a careful, well-planned manner), then we should be building at least two large publicly-owned refineries, one in the west and one in central Canada. If we can refine the sludge from Alberta ourselves, we'll create many more jobs and realize much more wealth from the resource. Let's stop importing oil that we won't need once we start refining and consuming more of our own. Given the state of the global environment, however, a far better option is phasing out tar sands oil production altogether while we actively seek and develop adequate, sustainable energy alternatives.

In the meantime, how can we explain Stephen Harper's inability to understand that any short-term economic gains that might be achieved through the blind pursuit of oil and gas production and export pale in comparison to the economic and human costs of the climate change nightmare that has already begun to descend upon us? Harper's record on the environment is not just appalling, it's irrational, shameful and catastrophic for our country and the world. Without a radical change in direction, extreme weather patterns are certain to continue to worsen until survival is our sole consideration.

— 3 —
HARPER'S WAR ON
OUR SCIENTISTS

O VER THE PAST five years, the government of Stephen Harper has dismissed more than 2,000 federally-funded government scientists. World-renowned research facilities have lost their funding, and hundreds of programs that monitored such matters as smoke stack emissions, food inspections, oil spills, water quality and climate change have experienced cuts or been shut down entirely. The government has even taken to dismantling scientific libraries.[1]

The assault on science and scientists in Canada has been constant and unrelenting under this regime. The common theme amongst commentators is that Stephen Harper's government is determined to ignore or suppress inconvenient facts, particularly those relating to the impacts of climate change or tar sands oil production.

In his book, *The War on Science*, journalist Chris Turner writes, "This is a government that does not simply ignore the best evidence but attempts to destroy the source of it, a government that does not merely disregard the advice of experts but prohibits them from speaking about their work in public." He calls it "a bureaucratic war on science, on reason—on the very foundations of enlightenment thought."[2] Turner says Harper's Conservatives have used three basic methods to undermine environmental stewardship in Canada: reduce the government's capacity to gather data; downsize or eliminate offices that monitor and analyze scientific information; and seize control of channels of scientific information and prevent the publication or release of any information that could interfere with government policy.

Nearly half of scientists responding to a 2013 Environics survey, commissioned by the Professional Institute of the Public Service of Canada, reported that they knew of cases of direct government suppression of scientific information. A quarter of government scientists reported that they had been asked to exclude or change technical information in their own documents. Many reported political interference in their scientific work which they said had compromised the health and safety of Canadians, and most did not believe they could state their concerns publicly, or to the media, without government retaliation.[3]

According to a *Maclean's* magazine story, one federal government scientist who, without permission from Ottawa, participated in a media interview about great white sharks was immediately reprimanded by a regional director: "talk to the media again without the explicit permission of the minister's office, and there (will) be serious consequences—like suspension without pay, or even dismissal."[4]

As is often the case, the media request to the scientist had come with just one day's notice. He duly sent an email to Ottawa but, receiving no response to what he considered an innocuous request, he went ahead with the interview only to be severely reprimanded after the fact.

Stories like this abound in Stephen Harper's Ottawa where Canada's top scientists have organized public demonstrations, appearing bound and gagged or in mock funeral procession to mark "the death of evidence." Remarkably, this kind of control and suppression of scientific information is something that most of us would expect to encounter in Russia or China or perhaps, at some periods in history, in the United States. Yet in December 2012, when the *Toronto Star* contacted scientists at NASA, Environment Canada and Natural Resources Canada for a story about the effects of climate change on the Arctic and Antarctic, "emails to the U.S. government scientists were personally returned, usually the same day and with offers to talk in person or by phone. Emails sent to Canadian government scientists led to apologetic responses that the request would have to be routed through public relations officials."[5] A leading American scientist with the Union of Concerned Scientists in Washington declared, "Canadian scientists are trying to figure out how to protect themselves from a government that is increasingly focused on message control over a more open discussion of the facts."[6]

A group of University of Waterloo academics wrote that "the federal government has severely degraded its internal scientific capacity, including its ability to perform and publicize its own scientific research, track outside scientific research, and monitor and assess policy issues with complex scientific content." They went on to say, "Whenever science seems likely to generate knowledge that could create difficulties for their political agenda, they try to bury the knowledge and destroy the government's capacity to generate it." It is "a willful effort to manufacture ignorance and a fundamental rejection of evidence-based public policy."[7]

The University of Victoria Environmental Law Centre put it succinctly: "There are few issues more fundamental to democracy than the ability of the public to access scientific information produced by government scientists—information that their tax dollars have paid for."[8]

The list of scientific facilities that the government has either closed or attempted to close across the country is exhaustive and growing. It includes research centers, monitoring centers, laboratories and even libraries. Here are just a few examples:

The Department of Fisheries and Oceans was forced to shut down laboratories that once monitored ocean pollutants, leaving us with next to no federal government capacity to monitor pollutants in the waters off our coasts.[9]

A world-renowned freshwater research institute was cut from the DFO budget in the government's 2012 omnibus budget bill. Its research station in Northern Ontario—known as the Experimental Lakes Area (ELA)—conducted critical research on such issues as the impact of acid rain, mercury and other contaminants, flame-retardants, and climate change on our abundant freshwater lakes. The public and scientific community raised the alarm at its imminent closure, and the facility was saved at the eleventh hour by funding from the International Institute for Sustainable Development and the governments of Ontario and Manitoba.[10]

There was also a planned shutdown of the Polar Environment Atmospheric Research Laboratory (PEARL), which tracks climate change and ozone depletion in the high Arctic. As one of the northernmost research stations, it monitored and reported conditions in the north that are key to understanding what is happening to the rest of the planet, and its threatened closure alarmed scientists worldwide.

PEARL had been supported with federal monies through the Canadian Foundation for Climate and Atmospheric Sciences, but in 2011 the Foundation's government funding came to an end. Researchers managed to find the means to operate the facility on a part-time basis for a year, although the financial shortfall meant gaps in its data. A grant through a new federal agency subsequently restored funding and its personnel are scrambling to restore its full operation and upgrade equipment.[11]

As mentioned in the previous chapter, Harper eliminated the National Roundtable on the Environment and the Economy, an independent body that advised federal and provincial governments on the projected costs of climate change in various economic sectors. Over a 25-year period, the Roundtable issued many reports on timber and energy production, water resources, air quality, the impact of coastal flooding, and more. It offered original ideas on integrating environmental conservation and economic growth, yet its funding was eliminated in the 2012 budget and it officially closed its doors in March of 2013.[12]

Some of our best known scientists claim that the consequences of all of this for Canada could be disastrous. Many departments of the federal government can no longer deliver the essential expert advice that not only once informed policy at home, but was automatically shared with the scientific community beyond our borders.

Criticism of the Harper government's attitude is now coming from international sources. In an open letter to Stephen Harper released in October 2014, more than 800 scientists from 32 countries, based at institutions ranging from the Harvard Medical School to the Max Planck Institute in Germany, decried "a rapid decline in freedoms and funding" for Canadian government scientists that made it more difficult for them to conduct research, communicate scientific information, and collaborate internationally. They wrote, "Canada's leadership in basic research, environmental, health and other public science is in jeopardy... We urge you to restore government science funding and the freedom and opportunities to communicate these findings internationally."[13]

Major international publications such as *The Guardian* and *The Economist* have called on the Harper government to take a more enlightened approach to scientific findings. Indeed, a contributor to one of the world's leading scientific journals, *Nature*, reported that, "increasingly we're hearing, 'all of my colleagues around the world know about what is going on and they simply can't understand what is happening in Canada'." A Canadian civil servant could only describe the situation as "absolutely embarrassing."[14]

In the spring of 2013, Canada's Federal Information Commissioner, Suzanne Legault, was presented with a 128-page report by the non-profit group, Democracy Watch and the Environmental Law Centre at the University of Victoria, and was asked to investigate allegations that Canada's government scientists were being muzzled. As of this writing, there is no known outcome of any investigation.[15]

Canada recently fell to number 20 in the World Press Freedom Index which measures the performance of a country's media.[16] The Index measures the degree of freedom that journalists and news organizations enjoy, as well as the efforts made by governments to protect this freedom. The scores are obtained through a questionnaire administered to journalists, researchers, jurists and human rights activists. In some cases, government permission had to be obtained by journalists before reporting information from Canadian scientists. And, as I previously mentioned, requests to interview scientists must now be channeled through public relations officials.

The government's indifference or outright antagonism to scientific research has extended even to libraries and priceless collections of books and research materials, including historical scientific data. *The Tyee* reported that "scientists say that the closure of some of the world's finest fishery, ocean and environmental libraries by the Harper government has been so chaotic that irreplaceable collections of intellectual capital built by Canadian taxpayers for future generations has been lost forever."[17]

While the government insists that all the valuable information from these dismantled libraries will be made available in a digitized format, photographic evidence of the ransacked shelves at Winnipeg's Freshwater Institute Library, one of the world's most comprehensive research libraries on freshwater biology, tell quite another story. Some scientists referred to the dismantling as being, "like a book burning."[18]

Reports of collections like that of the Maurice Lamontagne Institute Library in Mont-Joli, Quebec, found in dumpsters or sent to landfills, reveal a government that is at best careless with the historical and intellectual wealth of the nation, or worse, bent on the eradication of scientific knowledge. Even a former Fisheries minister in Brian Mulroney's cabinet, Tom Siddon, called the closings "Orwellian."[19]

Writing about another library's fate, Mark Bourrie recounted in the *Toronto Star* that, "despite paying for a consultant's report saying it was a bad idea, Health Canada shut down its Ottawa library last year [2013]. Books and journals, essential for serious research, were sent to the National Research Council"—a body which has been revamped to support industry, not science.

Bourrie noted that Health Canada used to employ 40 librarians and as of April, 2013, there were just 6. Scientists are increasingly unable to get assistance "from trained science librarians who know how to trace down rare and obscure publications."[20] A retired Health Canada pathologist, Rudy Mueller called it "an insidious plan to discourage people from using libraries. If you want to justify closing a library, you make access difficult and then you say it is hardly used."[21]

Peter Wells, a prominent marine environmental scientist at Dalhousie University and an aquatic toxicologist says, "The fact that many materials were thrown away or given away is heartbreaking to those of us who are dedicated to this field of research and the history of science in Canada. That we as a society are condoning information destruction and core library closures in Canada is unbelievable, and in my view, undemocratic and probably criminal."[22]

The actions of the Harper government remain inexplicable for most rational, thoughtful Canadians, though some have looked for an explanation in the evangelical fundamentalist religious bent of the Harper Conservatives' support base, particularly early Reform Party supporters. For this group, science itself is heresy, promoting the theory of evolution which they see as a threat to the concept of creation outlined in the book of Genesis. As Marci McDonald explains in her book, *The Armageddon Factor: The Rise of Christian Nationalism in Canada*, this group of social conservatives believes that God gave man "dominion" over the earth. For them, a phenomenon like climate change is not to be combatted but welcomed as a sign that the anticipated second-coming and Armageddon are at hand.[23]

The extent to which this kind of thinking is part of Harper's personal belief system or merely a condition favourable to an opportunistic political strategy, is something that I will leave you, the reader, to ponder. But McDonald's book is instructive on the influence of Christian fundamentalism on the Harper government.

Like McDonald, journalist Jeffrey Simpson does not discount that influence. He says, "If you want to understand the Harper government, never forget the Base. The prime minister doesn't. He can't afford to ignore it..." Simpson emphasizes that Harper's core voters exhibit "a high degree of religiosity, a moralistic view of foreign policy, a populist dislike of government, a loathing of the media except the Sun News Network, Sun newspapers and a few very right-wing columnists." They have "a reverence for the military, an abhorrence of abortion, a suspicion of 'intellectuals' and their reasoning, a belief (against all evidence) that crime is out of control, a generalized sense that honest, god-fearing people like themselves have been marginalized and patronized by 'secular' elites."[24]

Although much of this may baffle their fellow Canadians, what we do know with certainty is that Harper has launched an unprecedented attack on our scientists and on the facilities that support science in our country. The consequences are tragic.

— 4 —
HARPER'S TAX POLICE

I N 2012, STEPHEN HARPER's government began a systematic campaign, through the Canada Revenue Agency and through funding cuts, to disrupt and control the work of Canadian charities—in particular those working in the environmental field.

The offensive against some of Canada's most respected charities began shortly after a former aide to Conservative ministers Jason Kenney and John Baird, Alykhan Velshi, left his parliamentary job to join extreme far-right pundit Ezra Levant in founding a website called EthicalOil.org.[1] When Velshi returned to Parliament Hill in late 2011, he took a prominent job as the Director of Planning in the Prime Minister's Office.[2] Shortly after, EthicalOil.org began its attacks on Canada's charitable sector.

Officially, the EthicalOil.org website was established to promote tar sands oil as the "ethical, fair trade choice." Ironically, the website states: "Countries that produce Ethical Oil uphold human rights and have high environmental standards. They ensure economic justice and promote peace.

By contrast, Conflict Oil countries oppress their citizens and operate in secret with no accountability to voters, the press, or independent judiciaries."[3]

Once established, EthicalOil.org began targeting many noted environmental and non-profit groups, filing complaint after complaint with the Canada Revenue Agency about their activities. Soon after, an unprecedented number of "political activity audits" began of organizations across the country.

Allegations from organizations like Greenpeace that EthicalOil.org is simply a mouth-piece for the Harper government have been denied by the Conservatives, yet the facts suggest otherwise.[4]

Gareth Kirkby, a former journalist and graduate student in communications, studied this rash of audits for his master's thesis. He concluded that, "the data suggest that the current federal government is corrupting Canada's democratic processes by treating as political enemies those civil-society organizations whose contributions to public policy conversations differ from government priorities."[5]

Canadian Press reporter Dean Beeby prepared a revealing timeline of EthicalOil.org's complaints to the CRA and the agency's subsequent actions. It shows that a concerted campaign against certain Canadian charities began in January 2012, shortly after the release of an open letter from Joe Oliver, then Natural Resources minister, denouncing "environmental and other radical groups" who "threaten to hijack our regulatory system to achieve their radical agenda."[6]

Shortly after, in March 2012, EthicalOil.org filed a formal complaint to the CRA about the political activities of Environmental Defence Canada Inc.[7] Later that same month, the federal budget introduced new restrictions on the political activities of charities and demanded more disclosure of funding from foreign sources. The CRA was given an additional "$8 million over two years largely to establish a new political-activity audit program, with 10 such audits planned for the first fiscal year." The program was later expanded to a $13.4 million operation over a period of five years.[8]

Between April 2012 and March 2013, the first of 10 political-activity audits were initiated. At least five environmental charities—Environmental Defence Canada, Tides Canada Foundation, Tides Canada Initiatives Society, Ecology Action Centre, and Equiterre—were subjected to onerous tax audits.[9]

The Canadian Centre for Policy Alternatives, a policy think-tank that provides an important counterbalance to conservative institutions like the Fraser Institute and the C.D. Howe Institute, is among those undergoing the same process. It has long been on the radar of right-wing governments and is accustomed to attention from Revenue Canada. But this latest audit goes far beyond what they have experienced in the past. According to staffers, the current review is proving especially costly and time-consuming, causing serious disruption to the Centre's ongoing work.

Documents obtained under the Access to Information Act show that the CCPA was targeted by the CRA because the research and education material on its website was deemed by the CRA to be "biased" and "one-sided." Bruce Campbell, the CCPA's long-time executive director, says, "Under this definition, all think-tanks are biased or one-sided, and would not qualify for charitable status. The work of all think-tanks emanates from a set of values, progressive or conservative, that guide our research and policy analysis, and as such [may be termed] biased."[10]

According to Dean Beeby, "Among right-leaning or pro-business think-tanks in Canada, two—the C.D. Howe Institute in Toronto and the Macdonald-Laurier Institute in Ottawa—have confirmed to the *Canadian Press* they are not currently under audit for political activities. Two others—the Fraser Institute in Vancouver and the Montreal Economic Institute—have declined to comment on the matter."[11]

In April of 2012, EthicalOil.org was at it again, this time filing a formal complaint to the CRA about the David Suzuki Foundation. As a result, Suzuki, host of CBC TV's long-running program, "The Nature of Things," and one of Canada's best-known scientists, stepped down from the board of his own foundation to save it from allegations of political activity. Doing so allowed Suzuki to continue to express his views freely.[12]

The following month, Environment Minister Peter Kent made an outrageous blanket claim that Canadian charities had been used "to launder offshore funds for inappropriate use against Canadian interest"—that is, by obstructing the environmental assessment process.[13]

In July 2012, Physicians for Global Survival (PGS), originally incorporated as a charity in 1980 under the name Physicians for Social Responsibility, had its charitable status revoked for activities deemed "inherently political." The group was a long-standing peace organization, dedicated to making the world safe from nuclear weapons and war.[14]

By early 2014, it was apparent to organizations and media across Canada that a pattern was emerging amongst many of those targeted by the CRA. Then Finance Minister Jim Flaherty was questioned about why the government was auditing so many organizations that were opposed to pipeline projects. He responded by saying, "charities are not permitted to accept money from terrorist organizations."[15]

As of 2014, at least 52 political-activity audits of Canadian charities were underway. The scope of the CRA's review was broadened to include groups that fight poverty and human rights abuses, plus those promoting international aid.

According to the *Toronto Star*, CRA officials informed Oxfam Canada that "preventing poverty" was not an acceptable goal. Relieving poverty is legitimately charitable, but preventing it is not. "Preventing poverty could mean providing for a class of beneficiaries that are not poor." Oxfam Canada's executive director, Robert Fox, called the exchange he had with CRA officials an "absurd conversation." Fox said, "Their interpretation was that preventing poverty may or may not involve poor people."[16]

In July of 2014, three auditors showed up at the Toronto office of PEN Canada, the well-known freedom-of-expression body that represents more than 1,000 writers and supporters, including Canadian icons such as Margaret Atwood and Yann Martel.[17] PEN's website states: "PEN Canada is a nonpartisan organization of writers that works with others to defend freedom of expression as a basic human right, at home and abroad. PEN Canada promotes literature, fights censorship, helps free persecuted writers from prison, and assists writers living in exile in Canada."[18] In response to the audit, Margaret Atwood tweeted: "Now's the time to support PEN Canada, faced with a punishing audit by the Harper Conservatives. Why does the freedom of expression threaten them?"[19] According to the Dean Beeby, "The group has been highly critical of the Harper government in recent years for the muzzling of scientists on the public payroll, and for alleged spying on Canadian citizens in concert with U.S. eavesdropping agencies."[20]

In October 2014, the CRA focused its attention on the activities of the Kitchener-Waterloo Field Naturalists, a group of bird watchers who operate under a registered charity. They received a warning letter from tax auditors about political material on their website soon after the group wrote to two federal cabinet ministers, "complaining about government-approved chemicals that damage bee colonies." According to the CBC, the CRA's "stern missive says the group must take appropriate action as necessary 'including refraining from undertaking any partisan activities,' with the ominous warning that 'this letter does not preclude any future audits.'" Long-time member Roger Suffling, an adjunct professor at the University of Waterloo, believes that the warning—coming on the heels of their letters to the government—was no coincidence. "Effectively, they've put a gag on us," he says. "You can piece together the timing, the two things are very concurrent."[21]

Canada has descended into the politics of the absurd. Rick Mercer's portrayal of scientists hiding books from the government, or David Parkins' cartoon of birdwatchers being watched in turn through CRA binoculars makes for great comedy, but what is happening in Canada is nothing short of tragedy.

On the international front, it is no better. In addition to the chill imposed by the onslaught of political-activity audits, the Harper governments' defunding of programs and its amalgamation of the Canadian International Development Agency (CIDA) with Foreign Affairs and International Trade, has left many internationally-oriented charitable organizations mere shadows of what they once were—if they continue to exist at all.

CIDA was created in 1968 by Prime Minister Pierre Trudeau to administer foreign aid programs in developing countries and to operate in partnership with other Canadian and international organizations in the public and private sectors. It reported to the minister responsible for international development. The agency ceased to exist with Harper's 2013 budget bill, its functions subsumed by a new Department of Foreign Affairs, Trade and Development.[22] Along with this restructuring, the decades-old funding mechanism was changed. Organizations that could once depend on sustained annual core funding were suddenly required to submit bids for specific government projects.

Some organizations, like the Canadian Council for International Cooperation (CCIC), a national umbrella group for all the provincial councils and major development and aid organizations across the country, lost their funding even before the amalgamation took place. CCIC had received public funding for almost four decades, through successive governments, to support its work in strengthening Canada's non-governmental sector, as well as monitoring and analyzing federal policies on foreign affairs, aid, peace-building, trade and human rights. Gerry Barr, the head of CCIC, had protested federal defunding of a member-group, KAIROS, in late 2009. In July 2010, CCIC was advised that its government funding would be cut. For CCIC, "the decision was widely seen as payback for CCIC's advocacy of public policy positions that had run at cross-purposes to those of the government."[23]

The CCIC, like many of its member groups, had worked closely with the federal government for many years. They were the organizations on the frontlines in times of natural or humanitarian disasters, providing care and aid in Canada's name. They undertook anti-poverty and development work with partners overseas, ensuring that development funding was applied to projects in a fair, appropriate and accountable fashion.

Former prime ministers Paul Martin and Joe Clark, along with Ed Broadbent and one-time North-South Institute (NSI) director Joseph Ingram contributed an article to the *Globe and Mail* in September 2014 in which they lamented the loss of yet another major player in Canada's development sector.[24] They wrote: "The recent closing of the North-South Institute as a result of discontinued federal government funding is a loss both for Canada and for the global community. The closing of the NSI constitutes the jettisoning of a critically important tool of Canadian leadership internationally, exercised not through Canadian military or economic might, but rather through our capacity to generate and globally disseminate knowledge and best-practice alternatives. In 2011, 2012 and 2013, NSI was internationally recognized as the world's leading development policy think-tank with an annual budget of less than $3 million."

They continued, "Canada's aid levels are now amongst the lowest of the Organization for Economic Co-operation and Development (OECD) donors at about 0.2 percent of national income. And to follow this up with the progressive dismantling of the former CIDA and other publicly funded development institutions, such as Rights and Democracy, is beyond comprehension."[25]

According to figures released in October 2014, Canada's drop in foreign aid in 2013 was the largest reduction of any country in the OECD. The OECD report was released just as Foreign Affairs Minister John Baird was calling on Canadians to fight terrorism in Iraq, telling the House of Commons: "My Canada protects the vulnerable. My Canada does not leave the heavy-lifting to others." Baird's comments prompted University of Ottawa Professor Stephen Brown to observe, "We have a moral imperative for bombing, but not so much for helping the poor."[26]

Time and again, we find Stephen Harper at odds, literally and figuratively, with the values and traditions that have shaped our country. His government's assault on Canada's charitable sector reveals a regime determined to redefine not just the role of government, but the face of civil society itself.

For decades, the mosaic of organizations working on such critical issues as the environment, poverty, women's equality, aboriginal rights, and the well-being of children, both at home and abroad, have received public and private support for the initiatives they have undertaken on behalf of Canada and all of us. To suggest that these organizations are funded by terrorists, or to cripple their programs by abruptly eliminating their funding, or to use questionable tax audits to curtail and control their work is an affront to Canadians and another national and international embarrassment. There seem few limits on how far Stephen Harper is willing to go to impose his far-right vision on Canada.

Everything we value is at stake.

— 5 —

DATACIDE

NUMBERS CAN BE POWERFUL.
Numbers generated by credible organizations, based on careful data collection and sound research methods, allow for reliable measurements and comparisons. They express the irrefutable truth in ways that words alone often cannot. This is especially true when they are produced by highly respected institutions like Statistics Canada—or it was true before the Conservative government took aim at such institutions.

The OECD statistical comparisons that I have used for decades to chart economic and social changes in Canada against those in other OECD nations are often based on numerical data from Statistics Canada. These numbers help us understand how we are doing as a nation and where we stand in relation to the rest of the world. They allow governments to assess the effectiveness of social programs and determine where needs are unmet. They also assist social scientists, institutions and businesses to identify future needs and trends. In other words, reliable numbers can be the best ally of those who want to take the vital signs of our nation and respond appropriately. But for those whose agenda includes dismantling many of the support systems in Canadian society, numbers are the enemy, confirming an embarrassment of inconvenient truths.

Under the Harper government, we have seen not only disdain for unwelcome numbers but an active suppression of information gathering that is unprecedented in Canada.

In 1962, the Canadian government formed the National Council of Welfare, a non-partisan group whose cross-Canada members were appointed by the Governor-in-Council to advise the minister of Health and Welfare on issues relating to social welfare policy. The Council reported every year on the extent and depth of poverty in the country and its terrible consequences. It was a vital advisory body to successive governments, tracking the deprivation suffered by too many of our fellow citizens, examining approaches to poverty in other jurisdictions, and suggesting logical solutions to persistent problems.

Its reports were invaluable to researchers, anti-poverty groups, universities and provincial governments, economists, and legal and social service workers concerned with children and youth, aboriginal communities, income and security programs, employment programs, the tax system, etc. The reports covered a great range of issues related to poverty.

And yet with a single sentence buried in the 2012 omnibus budget, the Harper government shut down the Council with no public consultation and no advance warning. The savings to Ottawa was $1.1 million a year. The estimated cost of poverty in Canada is now some $30 billion a year.[1]

Writing in the *Toronto Star*, the former Council director, Steve Kerstetter declared, "The Conservative government's decision to scrap the Council in the budget speech was a cheap shot—in more ways than one—and a shot that will deprive Canadians of one more source of valuable research." He went on to say: "The Council's work on the welfare system has been extraordinary. Its annual publication *Welfare Incomes* is the single authoritative source on that subject in Canada and is used extensively both inside and outside government... Its reports on child poverty and women and poverty are well known. It has published some of the most readable descriptions of public and private pension programs. It documented the many shortcomings of legal aid in Canada... Also worth highlighting are the Council's reports on child care and its importance to young families."[2]

Kerstetter concluded, "The Conservatives didn't even have the decency to mention the demise of the Council in the budget speech. The budget papers included a table in one of the appendices that showed a cut of $1.1 million a year in the council's budget beginning next year. What the papers didn't bother to say was that $1.1 million was the Council's entire budget."[3]

Adding to the injury: only one Canadian newspaper reported this news of the Council's demise. Even the CBC overlooked it.

Could it be that the media was simply overwhelmed by the 400-page omnibus bill and they missed the line that axed the Council's budget? Or maybe they didn't realize that a $1.1 million "cut" eliminated the Council outright.

While it has successfully buried some sources of inconvenient numbers, the Harper government has effectively hobbled many others.

For years, Statistics Canada has been the most important data collection agency in the country, widely respected as one of the best statistical agencies in the world. No more. In 2010, the government decided to get rid of the very valuable national long-form census and replace it with a hopelessly inadequate National Household Survey.

Canada's mandatory long-form census was regarded as so fundamental to sound data collection that the agency's chief statistician, Munir Sheikh, resigned in protest in July, 2010. He referred to the long-form census as, "an anchor for surveys," calling on the government to bring it back and "restore sanity."[4] Carleton University Economics Professor Frances Woolley said, "There is nothing that kills social science research more quickly than lack of good data. If you want to kill social science research, the best thing to do is to destroy the data."[5]

The heart of knowledge-gathering in Canada has always been the census, especially the mandatory long-form questionnaire that collected information on such important factors as language, education, disability, landed immigrant status, citizenship, ability to speak official and other languages, ethnic or cultural origins, parents' place of birth, labour market activities, incomes and dwellings. Up until 2011, every fifth household was given the long-form questionnaire, while the short-form questionnaire went to the remaining 4 out of 5 households. Respondents to the long-form questionnaire, representing a significant 20 percent of the population, provided a pool of balanced data which underpinned future planning in myriad areas.

Imagine trying to run a household when you aren't sure how many mouths you have to feed, how many beds are required, who has health issues or disabilities that require special equipment and care, who will go to school, whether or not your vehicle is big enough to transport them, and how many additions to the family you might expect in the near future. Without such basic information, maintaining the household would be chaotic at best. A well-run country that adequately accommodates its population requires a similar knowledge of numbers and needs.

Without the mandatory long-form census, we are without that pool of essential data. Evidence from other countries shows that moving from a mandatory to a voluntary census hurts the vulnerable in particular: the poor, recent immigrants, and some minority groups. All segments of the population are less likely to respond to a survey that is "voluntary" rather than "mandatory," but the disadvantaged are less so inclined. This skews results and makes it more difficult to target programs where they are most needed.

The Harper government's decision to axe the mandatory long-form census grabbed media headlines and sparked a whirlwind of opposition from a wide range of institutions across Canada, from provincial governments and business, to academe and think-tanks, to banks and the volunteer sector. The change was denounced by the Statistical Society of Canada and the American Statistical Association. Ivan Fellegi, a former chief statistician who headed Statistics Canada for more than 20 years, said he could not remember a time that so many well-informed people and organizations became so vocal about a single issue.[6]

So draconian a measure might appear on the face of it to be motivated in part by financial considerations. But the reality is quite the opposite. Cancellation of the mandatory long-form census and its replacement by the voluntary National Household Survey actually cost more than the traditional census—a hefty $22 million more.[7]

This sum and more has been taken from the Statistics Canada budget with cuts estimated at $30 million over the two year period ending in April 2014, resulting in the loss of 767 jobs or 18 percent of the Statscan workforce.[8] It is projected that over 2,200 jobs will be eliminated by 2016, meaning that Statistics Canada will lose more than a third of its previous workforce.[9]

The impacts of these cuts and changes have been both damaging and wasteful.

One example: a 2012 Statscan labour skills survey of 25,000 companies to assess hiring needs and skill gaps ran out of money before the data from the survey could be analyzed and a report issued. A Statscan employee was quoted as saying that the survey could still be completed if someone "had the funding and wanted to carry it forward."[10] Up to that point the project had cost $4.6 million in taxpayers' money. The investment was completely wasted.

In July 2014, Statistics Canada incorrectly reported that only 200 new jobs had been created across Canada in the previous month, "signaling weakness in the economy" and resulting in a drop in the value of the Canadian dollar. The correct figure of 42,000 new jobs was released a few days later.[11] It was the most serious in a series of errors in recent years that many analysts have attributed to cutbacks and staff shortages, prompting a *Globe* editorial to call the government's cuts at Statscan a "false economy."[12]

The agency has made reductions to 34 of its programs and surveys.[13] Among the reports that have been cut are the invaluable *Survey of Labour Income and Dynamics*[14] and the much valued *Participation Activity Limitation Survey*, which sought to identify conditions and health issues that present barriers to Canadians' participation in the activities of daily life. *Social Security Statistics: Canada and the Provinces*, which has been described as a treasure-trove of information on federal, provincial/territorial and municipal government programs, has also disappeared. I myself once consulted two extremely valuable publications, *The Canadian Economic Observer* and *Canadian Social Trends*, on a monthly basis. Both relied on the long-form census for essential data and both are now gone, along with many other reports and studies.

The Harper government has tried to justify eliminating the mandatory long-form census with unfounded claims that large numbers of Canadians objected to the state's invasion of their privacy. Canada's privacy commissioner, however, says that in over ten years and two censuses, there were only three complaints on privacy grounds.[15]

(What many Canadians do object to is the involvement of the American firm Lockheed Martin, the world's largest manufacturer of weapons and maker of the F-35 fighter jet, in processing the Canadian census—a service for which it has been paid $81 million so far. This arrangement, which dates back to 2004, has angered many and prompted quite a few to refuse to participate in any census as long as Lockheed

Martin is engaged. In 2011, the mandatory short-form census had an impressive 98 percent compliance rate amongst Canadians. Some 54 non-respondents were prosecuted for refusing to complete it, several of whom were conscientious objectors due to Lockheed Martin's involvement.[16])

Today, Canadian researchers are saying that the damage from the cancelled long-form census is as serious as they feared. The new Household Survey data is unreliable and the impact is being felt by more than just researchers and academics: everyone from city planners to public health agencies are reporting that the 2011 census data is inadequate.[17] They warn of the "harmful implications for public policy" and of data quality that is "masking key shifts in income inequality and poverty," creating a distorted picture that has left them unable to track trends over time. The new survey, at a total cost of $652 million, amounts to a waste of taxpayer dollars that could result in misguided policy decisions.[18]

"We're concluding that it pretty much is garbage," said one University of Toronto expert.[19] Others have warned against using the material, calling it not only unreliable but dangerous. Researcher and economist Armine Yalnizyan listed just a few of the implications for census users, including the inability to make informed decisions in such critical areas as these:

- future extensions of public transit;
- where to target different types of health resources;
- how to prioritize emergency response;
- where the best educational outcomes are occurring and what drives the differences;

- the greatest needs for after-school programs, immigrant and child care service;

Further, she cited the likelihood that:

- Canadian entrepreneurs won't be able to target the best markets for launching new products;
- Investors will not know where supply is heading without reliable data on the changing demographics of the marketplace;
- Charities won't be sure if they are addressing today's needs or tomorrow's problems.[20]

Economists at some of our largest financial institutions have also spoken out. According to David Parkinson of the *Globe and Mail*, Benjamin Tal, deputy chief economist at CIBC World Markets, has "decried the deplorable lack of statistical detail that has left us with only a partial, hazy picture of the health (or lack thereof) of Canada's housing sector." Says Parkinson: "We don't know how much of the booming condo market is made up of foreign investors. We don't know the credit quality of the borrowers who are receiving mortgages, and how many are behind in their payments. We can't tell the average size of a down payment. Without that, it's awfully hard to conclude whether the big numbers—such as housing starts, sales prices—reflect a strong market, a high-risk asset bubble, or anything in between."[21]

He goes on to warn that, "housing is just one of the places where we are suffering a disturbing dearth in statistical data that could answer some crucial questions about our economy and provide critical guidance to future policy." He names others: the labour force, employment and under-employment, business investment, business formation, and more.[22]

As recently as February 2015, the mayors of 19 of Canada's largest cities, meeting at the Big Cities Summit, cited the loss of the mandatory long-form census data as a critical issue in municipal planning. They say that without adequate demographics on such things as ethnicity and low-income, they are unable to adequately address the challenges.[23]

In a note to me in June 2014, Ken Battle, president of the Caledon Institute of Social Policy in Ottawa, articulated the over-arching dangers of what he calls "data vandalism." He wrote, "Information is the life-blood of sound public policy and good government. Without comprehensive, reliable statistics, policy-making will be done in the dark... Without comprehensive information, Canadians are susceptible to the myths, misconceptions and half-truths that persist in science and social policy. Without an understanding of how programs operate governments can get away with 'social policy by stealth'... Unfortunately, information is under attack in Ottawa. Canadians are facing a new and insidious threat from their very own federal government—datacide."[24]

In short, under the Harper government, we have suffered a deliberate and relentless assault on the gathering, recording and dissemination of information that is essential to measuring and monitoring the vital signs of our nation. We are left ill-equipped to meet the needs of Canadians now and in the future. What we are witnessing is the systematic dismantling of the statistical and informational foundation necessary for a stable and healthy democratic nation.

— 6 —

NEGLECT OF THE
POOR AND VULNERABLE

MORE THAN TWENTY-FIVE years after the House of Commons unanimously resolved to end child poverty in Canada by the year 2000, the country's record remains a national disgrace—one that has only grown worse under Stephen Harper.

According to UNICEF's *Report Card 10*, Canada's child poverty rate sat at 14 percent in 2012, placing us 24th out of 35 industrialized countries. In 2013, UNICEF reconfirmed the 14 percent rate, pointing out that half the countries in their survey of comparable affluent nations achieved a relative child poverty rate below 10 percent. And, in its latest *Report Card 12* (2014), UNICEF noted that while Canada weathered the recession of 2008-11 better than most, "the child poverty gap widened by two percentage points as the most vulnerable slipped further into poverty."[1]

In terms of our overall poverty rate, the OECD Factbook 2014, places us 23rd out of the 34 OECD countries.[2]

Campaign 2000, a non-partisan coalition of anti-poverty groups and institutions, reported in 2012 that "with more children living in poverty today than in 1989 [the year of the House resolution], the case for federal action to end child poverty is clear. Most recent statistics indicate that 979,000 or 14.5% of children in Canada live in poverty as of 2010, compared to 912,000 or 13.7% in 1989."[3]

In 2009, the Senate of Canada unanimously endorsed its long-awaited standing committee report on poverty in Canada, *In From the Margins: A Call to Action on Poverty, Housing and Homelessness*. Two years in the making, it was based on testimony provided during more than 35 hearings, five roundtables, and site visits to 20 agencies in nine cities across Canada. The Senate committee heard from more than 175 witnesses, "some living in poverty and/or homeless themselves, others working for community agencies, and some analysts from universities, think tanks and national voluntary organizations."[4]

The report concluded that "far too many Canadians living in cities live below any measure of the poverty line; that too many people struggle to find and maintain affordable housing; and that an increasing number of Canadians are homeless." And, "despite the thoughtful efforts and many promising practices of governments, the private sector, and community organizations that are helping many Canadians, the system that is intended to lift people out of poverty is substantially broken, often entraps people in poverty, and needs an overhaul."[5]

Tom Gribbons, chair of Vibrant Communities Saint John, told the committee that: "Fundamentally, people do not want to live better in poverty, they want to get out of poverty... We need better measures to help us understand the economic cost of poverty and the economic benefit of helping particularly our children and young families to get out of poverty. Although people want to do social good, we are even more compelled to act when the business case is made that poverty reduction means that some form of economic gain will be there for all."[6]

The Senate report contained 72 comprehensive recommendations for addressing poverty and homelessness in Canada, including such measures as a national housing and homelessness strategy; an increase in the National Child Benefit; a nationwide federal/provincial initiative on early childhood learning; a basic annual income; a basic income floor for all disabled Canadians; and a rise in welfare benefits to at least the low-income cut-off. In the Foreword to the report, Committee chairs Art Eggleton and Hugh Segal stated: "We need—once and for all—to break the cycle of poverty in Canada, and to finally lift its devastating burden. We owe it to the millions of Canadians that struggle day in day out with poverty. But we also owe it to Canada as whole. The time for action is now."[7]

How did Stephen Harper respond? His government simply rhymed off a list of so-called accomplishments in reducing poverty without directly responding to a single recommendation contained in the report. To many observers, it was a shameful performance. Two years of remarkable effort by the Senate, by individual Canadians, by institutions and groups across the country who gave their best to help resolve a critical national issue, was dismissed and ultimately ignored. Ironically, just a month earlier on November 4th, 2009, an all-party resolution had passed in the House, calling on the government to develop an immediate plan to eliminate poverty in Canada.

The response to the Senate report should probably come as no surprise given the Harper government's similar treatment of the historic Kelowna Accord, widely viewed as an unprecedented agreement between the previous federal government, the provinces and Canada's Aboriginal people. The Accord was the culmination of eighteen months of meetings and laid out what was essentially a detailed roadmap for the strengthening of relationships between First Nations and governments, with measures to finally address the abject conditions in which far too many Aboriginal Canadians live. Four of every ten indigenous children currently live in poverty and in First Nations communities where the federal government is the primary funder, one out of every two children lives in poverty.[8]

Today, the Kelowna Accord represents a lost opportunity of tragic proportions. It was signed on November 25th, 2005 and abandoned soon after Stephen Harper took office with his first minority government in January, 2006. It committed 5 billion dollars over a 5 year period with specific, mutually-agreed targets for improvements in housing, potable water, education, healthcare, etc.

Without the meaningful action the Accord promised, Stephen Harper's (2008) apology for the abuses of the residential school system and the establishment of the Truth and Reconciliation Commission, and his signing of the UN Declaration on the Rights of Indigenous Peoples in 2010, seem hollow gestures.

The government's failure to take meaningful action on the missing and murdered Aboriginal women, its one-size-fits-all First Nations Education Bill, and controversial demands for financial accountability, represent major setbacks from the goal of moving beyond the mistakes of the past. Writing in the *Toronto Star*, Tim Harper says of the First Nations Financial Transparency Act: "In reality, there was no compelling need for such legislation, especially from a government that had once championed its own transparency and accountability and now demands it of all but itself." [9]

Why would Stephen Harper walk away from a landmark agreement like the Kelowna Accord? Well, for starters, it was a Liberal achievement.

The advantages of a healthy population and a robust workforce impacts every aspect of Canadian life, helping to create a thriving economy. Our calculation of the costs of poverty must include not just the social costs, but the terrible price of lost opportunities and contributions from those who remain on the margins of the country's economy.

Seth Klein and Armine Yalnizyan of the Canadian Centre for Policy Alternatives say that poverty should not be considered unavoidable in a society as wealthy as ours, and that the experience of such nations as England, Sweden and the Netherlands show the efficacy of bold government policies. They ask, "By what twisted economic logic, in a nation with a total annual income of about $1.6 trillion, are we allegedly unable to afford to take a serious run at the poverty in our midst, knowing the payoff from these initiatives will benefit citizens and public treasuries for years to come?" [10]

This government's bold policy? By cancelling the mandatory long form census in 2010, it eliminated one of the most important instruments for measuring poverty rates in Canada. Campaign 2000, along with many other anti-poverty organizations, has decried the lack of detailed, reliable data for tracking and analyzing poverty rates, especially among minority, Aboriginal, immigrant and disability communities.[11]

In my previous book, *The Truth About Canada*, I examined the tragedy of poverty in Canada, detailing the soaring numbers who must resort to food banks and the fact that a high percentage of those who rely on them are children. The situation is not improving. A November 2014 editorial in the *Toronto Star* cited research findings that 841,000 people had visited a food bank in March of 2014, up 25 per cent from 2008, the beginning of the last major economic downturn. Of those, 87,533 people were using food banks for the first time and 37 per cent of the total were children. Food banks are increasingly serving singles (43 per cent of the total, up from 29 per cent in 2001) and males. Concluded the *Star*, "All of this is completely unnecessary in a country as wealthy as Canada."[12]

There seems no shortage of funding available for the multi-billion dollar purchase of F-35 fighter-jets, or for engaging in the latest military adventure, even as the government drags its feet on providing the essentials that an increasing number of Canadians—children in particular—desperately need.

Despite record-breaking profits in much of the corporate sector, the ranks of the working poor continue to rise steadily. Even middle-class wages and salaries have stagnated and the prosperity that was supposed to flow from Canada's low corporate taxes has failed to materialize for most citizens.

Beyond such essentials as adequate housing, food, and dental care, the children of the working poor are too often unable to access quality daycare or the programs and activities that provide the socialization and skill development to help ensure they grow up as healthy, contributing members of society. According to a CIBC-sponsored poll conducted by Northstar Research Partners in June 2014, "one third of Canadian children, aged three to 17, do not participate in organized sport largely due to cost, a staggeringly high number at a time when youth obesity is on the rise."[13] Ed Broadbent later commented, "Low-income families cannot afford to buy their kids hockey equipment, enroll them in piano lessons or pay the cost of school trips... The growing gap between the poor and the middle-class, let alone the top 1 per cent, flies in the face of the democratic ideal that all children should have equal opportunities to develop their talents and capacities to the full."[14]

Countries that have successfully reduced their poverty rates have applied aggressive national strategies at different levels of government and across departmental bureaucracies. They have moved away from benefits-only poverty reduction measures, implementing instead broad-based policies that support long-term programs like jobs training and child care.

In its 2006 budget, the Harper government walked away from Canada's fledgling national child care system, and replaced it with the Universal Child Care Benefit, which provides $100 per month for every child under the age of six. Even with later slight enhancements, this did little to help families find child care in communities where wait lists can sometimes extend to years. Nor did it substantially ease the

$700-$1600 per month fees that many daycares charge. For those unable to access child care due to lack of availability or affordability, nothing changed.

A national housing strategy is another measure long demanded by anti-poverty activists. Not only has the Harper government failed to develop such a strategy, in 2011 it reduced the budget of the Canadian Mortgage and Housing Corporation by one-third. According to CMHC, "the number of households assisted under federal housing programs will be cut by almost 100,000 to fall from 623,700 household in 2008 to 525,000 household in 2016." This comes at a time "when most communities across Canada report that the aftershocks from the 2008 recession are continuing to cause deep housing and homelessness distress... Toronto's affordable housing wait list has set a new record every month, year after year, since the fall of 2008."[15]

Between now and 2018, housing cooperatives across the country are expected to lose the subsidies that provided affordable housing for those unable to pay full market rates. Most operated on the principle that affordable housing should not exceed 30 percent of income and rents were geared accordingly. Mass evictions are feared as federal government subsidies come to an end, affecting some of Canada's most vulnerable citizens, especially those living on disability pensions.[16]

Affordable housing and child care are fundamental needs that must be addressed if we are to build a stable foundation for all Canadians. When a family's housing costs are too high and daycare unaffordable, the effects can be catastrophic. If you cannot earn enough to afford child care, you cannot work. Without adequate and secure housing, long-term employment is more challenging, if not impossible. It's that simple.

Meanwhile, the Conservatives' offer up such one-off initiatives as a deeply flawed income-splitting plan. Announced in late 2014 to make good on a 2011 election promise, the scheme will cost the country $2 billion a year and deliver no benefit at all to single parents. The maximum benefit will be enjoyed primarily by high income, traditional families.[17] Federal cash benefits to assist low-income families have not been increased for seven years.

Repeated calls for enlightened federal leadership on poverty reduction have been loud and clear, yet apparently unheard and certainly unheeded by the Harper government. Among the most eloquent was *The Dollars and Sense of Solving Poverty* (2011), from the now defunct National Council of Welfare. "The costs and consequences of poverty are much larger than direct spending on social programs. We see the total costs when indirect and societal costs are taken into account...The Council urged a preventative approach that would result in significant savings in health care, prisons, shelters and other social services, and touted the benefits of reduced pressure on hospitals, higher levels of literacy and numeracy and a healthier workforce—all of which would benefit the economy.[18]

Senator Art Eggleton lamented, "Poverty is a hard sell. It shouldn't be, because it costs everybody. Our future prosperity may well depend on how we address our current level of poverty. I quite simply don't believe we can afford poverty anymore."[19]

Among the vulnerable in our midst, we must include recent immigrants and refugees who come to Canada in desperate circumstances. The list of measures taken against these individuals is a sorry litany, starting with the Harper government's 2012 decision to cut back on health benefits for immigrants, rejected refugee claimants, and those from "safe" countries. The organization Canadian Doctors for Refugee Care took the government to court on procedural and Charter grounds, where they won a partial but significant victory. In a Federal Court ruling in July 2014, Justice Anne Mactavish, deemed the cuts "cruel and unusual" treatment and unconstitutional. Furthermore, she said, they put at risk "the very lives of these innocent and vulnerable children in a manner that shocks the conscience and outrages our standards of decency." She gave the government four months to restore the health care funding.[20] The government said it would appeal.

Canada and the United States are the only countries that make refugees repay their travel and medical costs. And Canada is the only country that charges interest—prime plus one per cent. According to the Canadian Council for Refugees, when the Federation of Canadian Municipalities called on the government to absorb the cost of refugee transportation loans, then Minister for Citizenship, Immigration and Multiculturalism Jason Kenney responded, "The answer is 'no'... Canada is grappling with a deficit and like the world economy in general, is still recovering from a global recession. The government of Canada is committed to balancing the books."[21]

Balancing the books on the backs of frightened and traumatized refugees who have fled violence and persecution and usually arrive with little more than the clothes they are wearing. Government-assisted refugees are required to begin repaying their transportation loans within 30 days of arriving in Canada. With professional credentials that are not always recognized and frequent language barriers, most struggle in extreme stress and poverty, unable to find gainful employment. They require access to strong societal supports to ensure that they are not permanently relegated to the ranks of our country's poor.

Another recent change to Canada's immigration law, enacted in July 2014, lowered the age of dependent immigrant and refugee children from 21 to 18, with no exceptions. Dependent children can be automatically accepted along with their parents under Canada's immigration rules; this change disqualifies those older than 18. A *Toronto Star* editorial blasted the move: "the government says it wants to bring the definition of dependent children in line with the Canadian standard. Never mind that more than 43 per cent of our 20-somthings still live at home or that so many other young adults are otherwise dependent on their parents."[22] Dare we ask how any of this fits with the "family values" agenda of the Harper Conservatives?

A final, telling example. In October 2013, the *Toronto Star* reported the story of a family of six who had been denied refugee status by Canada's Immigration and Refugee Board and deported back to Libya in 2008. "Upon arrival at the airport in Libya, Adel Benhmuda, the father in the family, was imprisoned and tortured. The family eventually fled to Malta and lived in a shipping container in a refugee camp. In January 2013—after a Federal Court slammed

Canadian immigration officials for treating the Benhmuda case unfairly—the federal government agreed to let them back into Canada on humanitarian grounds." But Canadian officials insisted that the family pay the $6,000 it had cost the government to deport them to Libya in 2008, before they could apply for a federal transportation loan to return to Canada.[23] Following a public outcry, this demand was eventually rescinded.

It's difficult to characterize the Harper government's conduct more precisely than the Federal Court justice: "cruel and unusual treatment" that "shocks the conscience and outrages our standards of decency." Our once admirable immigration and refugee system is becoming a cruel joke, and Stephen Harper's austerity is transforming a caring and compassionate country into a suspicious and heartless place. As the former head of the Privy Council, Alex Himelfarb, has observed, austerity has yielded a "trickle-down meanness."[24]

— 7 —
UNFAIR, UNEQUAL, UNJUST
INCOME AND WEALTH IN
STEPHEN HARPER'S CANADA

IN *THE TRUTH ABOUT CANADA*, I wrote extensively about the problem of income distribution and inequality in Canada, a phenomenon that has accelerated dramatically under Stephen Harper.

The widening gap in salary and compensation levels among Canadian wage earners has aroused considerable attention and debate in recent years. But it turns out that disparities in wealth distribution—or more precisely, wealth concentration—are even more extreme than those of income distribution.

A 2014 study by the Broadbent Institute found that between 2005 and 2012, the poorest 10 percent of Canadians saw their net worth fall by an astounding 150 percent—meaning that they had more debt than assets and hence a negative net worth. During the same period, Canada's wealthiest 10 percent enjoyed an increase in their net worth of 42 percent.[1]

The top 20 percent of Canadians control 67.4 percent of all wealth in Canada while the poorest 20 percent of Canadians own no share at all.[2] Overall, there has been a significant deterioration of wealth among the lowest 30 percent of Canadians. Rick Smith, director of the Broadbent Institute commented, "There are so many people being left behind and there is simply no excuse for this deep and persistent wealth inequality in Canada."[3]

Also in 2014, a senior economist at the Canadian Centre for Policy Alternatives, David Macdonald, released an analysis of wealth distribution titled *Outrageous Fortune: Documenting Canada's Wealth Gap*. Quoting from his findings:

Canada's richest 20 percent of families take almost 50 percent of all income. But when it comes to wealth, almost 70 percent of all Canada's wealth belongs to Canada's wealthiest 20 percent.

In Canada ... wealth has flowed into the hands of a concentrated few... In 2012, according to figures derived from *Canadian Business* magazine, the 86 wealthiest Canadian-resident individuals (and families) held the same amount of wealth as the poorest 11.4 million Canadians combined.

The Wealthy 86 could buy up all of New Brunswickers' 545,000 motor vehicles, all of their 314,000 houses and cottages, all of their undeveloped land, all of their stocks and bonds, all of their pension funds, all of their RRSPs, all of their jewellry and all of their furniture. The Wealthy 86 have enough money to buy absolutely everything in the private hands of every New Brunswicker, with billions of dollars to spare.

The wealthiest quintile [that is, the wealthiest 20 percent of Canadians], held 67 percent of all wealth in 2012 . . .
the poorest three quintiles were largely unchanged in the
proportion of wealth they held since 1999.

In 2012, the Wealthy 86 represented roughly 0.002
percent of all the people in Canada while managing to accu-
mulate $178 billion in net worth.[4]

Both the Broadbent Institute survey and the CCPC report
pointed to the fact that the wealth disparity gap was overwhelmingly underestimated by Canadians or went largely
unnoticed, yet it is a critical measure of economic and social
well-being in an industrialized society.

Now let's turn to the more commonly studied issue of
income distribution. In the mid-1990s Canada was ranked
the 14th "most equal" in income distribution within the
group of OECD countries. Today, Canada is ranked well
down the list at 22nd. During a period in which 15 other
OECD nations managed to reduce their rates of inequality,
Canada tumbled from above average to below average.

Addressing the House of Commons Standing Committee on Finance in April 2013, economist Armine Yalnizyan
presented these facts and told committee members, "The
economic pie has more than doubled, yet the share of Canadians with inflation-adjusted earnings between $30,000 and
$60,000—what could be termed the 'middle class'—contin-
ues to decline." Furthermore, "by 2010, over 50 percent of
Canadians earned less than $30,000, a slightly larger share
of the working population than in the mid-1970s in inflation-adjusted terms."[5]

This trend is so serious that in early 2013 even the Conference Board of Canada weighed in, warning that if left unchecked income inequality will lead to lost potential, increased costs, squandered opportunity and potential social instability. Using the "Gini co-efficient," which measures the extent to which income distribution deviates from perfectly equal distribution, Canada was given a "C" grade and placed 12th out of 17 western-industrialized countries. Denmark, Norway, Belgium, Finland and Sweden topped the list in that order, receiving an "A," while the United States ranked last with a "D."[6]

The TD Bank likewise issued a warning about the costs of increasing income inequality. In a report published in November 2014, it stated, "While Canada's track record is better than the United States, Canada has experienced a significant rise in inequality over the past several decades. Moreover, a number of trends suggest that income inequality may rise higher, and social mobility could decline, in the years ahead."[7]

As early as November of 2011, Canada 2020, a progressive, non-partisan think tank that focuses on long-term federal policy issues, issued a report entitled: *Reducing Income Disparities and Polarization*. It pointed to growing income polarization as a fundamental challenge for Canada, a problem that can have "seriously perverse effects on both the economy and on society. At an extreme, it can undermine social cohesion, unravelling the fabric of a country."[8]

More recently, Dennis Raphael, a professor of Health Policy and Management at York University, and Toba Bryant, an assistant professor in Health Sciences at the University of Ontario Institute of Technology, linked income inequality with the premature deaths of 40,000 Canadians every year. Using data from Statistics Canada, they concluded that "income inequality is not only bad for our quality of life and economic productivity, it is directly related to the deaths of Canadians on an almost unimaginable scale." [9]

One of the major drivers behind increased inequality in both income and wealth in Canada has been our low corporate tax rate. Back in 2000, Canada's corporate tax rate was 28 percent. Under the Liberals, it was reduced to 21 percent. And effective January 1, 2012, under the Harper Conservatives, it was dropped to an all-time low of just 15 percent. According to a 2014 Canadian Labour Congress study, the federal government collected $34.9 billion in corporate income tax revenues in 2012-13, based on a corporate income tax rate of 15%. If the rate was still at 21%, where it was when the Harper government took office, revenue in that year would have been $13 billion higher. [10]

We have been told for decades that lowering corporate taxes would benefit Canadians and the economy; that companies would reinvest their increased profits in research and development—in new factories, new machinery and equipment, and into training to improve productivity. We were promised this would create more and better jobs, and boost economic growth and productivity.

But it hasn't happened. Many corporations have simply increased the dividends paid to shareholders. There has been an unprecedented surge in the pay of top corporate executives, even as salaries for lower-level employees have stagnated. And, says the CLC, many companies have become "cash hoarders," holding on to cash as a financial asset. [11]

Despite all the rhetoric we've been fed, the truth is that corporate tax cuts have benefitted only the wealthy and have encouraged a new level of self-serving greed within the corporate elite. Yet Conservatives and right-wing pundits and think tanks continue to espouse the benefits of lower taxes despite overwhelming evidence to the contrary.

The share of taxes paid to provincial and federal governments by corporations in Canada, as a share of overall government revenues, has been continually decreasing. Reduced government revenues not only mean continuing government deficits but, more critically, severe cuts to social programs such as unemployment insurance, job and skills training, and healthcare, leaving enormous holes in the economic and social safety net that once assisted low and medium wage earners.

The proportion of unemployed who now qualify for regular Employment Insurance benefits, for example, has dropped dramatically. The *Toronto Star* reported in 2012 that, "currently, only 40 per cent of the unemployed nationally qualify for Employment Insurance benefits, but the government feels some EI recipients are taking advantage of the system and passing up local job opportunities. Under the proposed changes [introduced in 2013], unemployed Canadians will for the first time be required to look for a job every day they receive benefits and be able to show evidence of their job search.[12]

The Canadian Labour Congress responded by pointing out that as a result, unemployed Canadians are being forced to look for jobs that do not exist or they risk losing the EI benefits they've paid for. They must be prepared to take lower paying jobs or jobs for which they are over-qualified, if located within an hour's travel time.[13]

More of the jobs currently being created in Canada are part-time positions that offer inadequate pay and few benefits, and which leave workers ineligible to receive EI benefits. In 2014, Tavia Grant reported in the *Globe* that "part-time work accounted for 80 percent of net job creation in the past year" and that part-time employees make up close to one-fifth (19.3 percent) of the Canadian workforce. At least 1 million of these part-time employees would choose full-time employment, if it were available. Many part-time workers cite concerns over job security, the lack of adequate benefits, irregular shifts and hours worked—all of which create stress and have serious implications for financial planning, childcare, and educational pursuits.[14]

This combination of too many part-time, low-paying jobs plus harsh cutbacks to essential social programs has created a perfect storm of inequality in our country. According to Canada 2020 in 2011, "More than half of low-income households in Canada can be classified as 'working poor.'"[15] And the situation is not improving.

Was no one in Ottawa paying attention or did they not care? Either way, the widening gaps in the distribution of income and wealth in Canada is disgraceful, as well as dangerous for Canada's future.

Armine Yalnizyan says it best: "Rising inequality, in good times and bad, makes it increasingly feel like the game is rigged, destabilizing foundational values and expectations ... A system that lets a small group gain more while the majority is forced to settle for less, despite ever-greater effort, is a prescription for trouble. No one knows the tipping point, but lock enough people out of the promise of gains and at some point, instead of stability and growth, you get social unrest." [16]

Those without resources can no longer effectively participate in the economic life of the nation. They are marginalized and ultimately feel disenfranchised, creating a ripple effect in the economy and in society.

It is time to restore sanity to economic and political governance. Canada should work for all Canadians. We cannot continue to allow our nation to be a piggy bank for the privileged few.

— 8 —
MISMANAGEMENT
OF THE ECONOMY, PART 1:
LOSING OUR COMPETITIVE EDGE

I N A *GLOBE AND MAIL* article in September 2014, business writer David Parkinson reported that the World
Economic Forum (WEF) had ranked Canada 15th out
of 144 countries in its Global Competitiveness Report for
2014–15. It was a drop of one notch from Canada's 14th place
finish the year before, which might not have been alarming
but for the fact that this latest score was Canada's lowest
since Harper took power in 2006.

Global competitiveness is a key indicator of our economic
future as a nation and a forecast of our future prosperity. The
WEF's index measures twelve factors that influence a country's global competitiveness, including financial market
development, labour market efficiency, technological read-
iness, innovation, and business sophistication—all of which
impact productivity and our ability to compete in the global
economy. The Conference Board of Canada is a partner

in producing these annual competitiveness reports, and the numbers are usually presented at the World Economic Forum's annual meetings.

According to the WEF and the Conference Board, Canada is performing well below the highest ranked countries on key economic indicators such as productivity and innovation. Switzerland was at the top of the 2014–15 list for the second year in a row thanks to its excellent innovation record and a sophisticated business culture, followed by Singapore. The United States moved up two positions to third place, with Finland, Germany and Japan close behind.

Parkinson wrote, "As recently as 2009, Canada was ranked 9th in the WEF's annual ratings, as its financial-system stability and relative economic health gave it a considerable competitive advantage over many of its badly wobbling global peers. But as the world's economy and financial system has recovered, Canada's position in the rankings has eroded."[1]

A year earlier, the Science, Technology and Innovation Council (an 18-member panel established by the Harper government to replace various other science advisory bodies) had highlighted one of the reasons for Canada's lackluster showing. *Globe* science reporter Ivan Semeniuk cited the Council's findings that, "without more support for industry and investment in research and development, Canada will be hard pressed to keep up with international competition and will risk an erosion of its economic well-being." How is that going to happen with Harper's attacks on our scientific community?

The Council identified a number of R&D-related factors that show where Canada is falling behind: "the number of doctorates awarded in science and technology relative to the total population; the fraction of Canadians working in science and technology; support for research in academic institutions; R&D investment by the private sector; and spending on information and communication technology in support of innovation." It found that Canada had slipped from 16th to 23rd among industrialized countries in overall expenditures on research and development relative to GDP, and it recommended more direct government support for industry-driven research rather than "indirect support in the form of tax credits." Howard Alper, the chair of the Council and a chemistry professor at the University of Ottawa, said, "We continue to face challenges as an innovation nation. This has to change if we are to compete well internationally and secure a strong future."[2]

Although the terms "research and development" (R&D), "innovation" and "productivity" are often used interchangeably in discussions of global competitiveness, it is research and development that drives new technology and innovation. These in turn drive productivity and determine our global competitiveness. Canada's failure to adequately invest in R&D is a major contributor to our decline in productivity and competitiveness in the global economy.

For years, I've pointed out that Canada's business community isn't spending as much as it should on R&D as a percentage of gross domestic product (GDP). In fact, Canadian businesses commit proportionately less to R&D than their peers in most other developed countries. According to the OECD's 2012 economic survey of Canada, the business sector "devotes only about 1% of GDP to R&D, compared with 2% in the U.S. and more than 2.5% in Japan, Korea and

some of the Nordic countries. Canada remains a low per-
former on business investment in R&D, even when the large
share of natural resource production is taken into account."[3]
Canada ranks in the bottom third of OECD countries in terms
of business spending on R&D, and our productivity growth
rate is less than half the OECD average. Inflation-adjusted
R&D, in constant dollars, has fallen for the last six consecutive years for which data is available.[4]

A 2012 Conference Board of Canada assessment concurs:
we're in 13th place when we measure our innovation performance against a group of 16 peer countries, and rate no more
than a "D" grade on innovation, on business R&D spending,
and on patents.[5]

Patents are a useful barometer of innovation, a measure of
how well a nation transforms knowledge into usable inven-
tions. The more patents a country has, the more likely it is to
develop new technology, to "derive above-average economic
gain from its intellectual property," in the words of the OECD.
That organization records another less than stellar performance in the patent category. In the OECD Factbook 2014,
we rank 18th amongst OECD countries in terms of triad
patent applications (those patents submitted for the same
invention to patent offices in the U.S., the EU and Japan) per
population, behind Japan, Switzerland, Sweden, Germany,
Finland, the Netherlands, Denmark and the United States,
amongst others.[6]

Canada has one of the lowest rates of direct government
funding of business R&D within the OECD.[7] Good economic
governance demands government involvement to provide
incentives for Canadian businesses to invest in our economic

future. We have decades of evidence to show that simply offering lower corporate tax rates is not the answer—it has produced precisely the opposite result. Clearly this has to change.

Don Drummond is a former associate deputy minister of Finance and former chief economist at TD Financial Group. In 2011, he wrote that low productivity had been a concern of Canadian economists in recent decades: "In the 1950s and 1960s, Canada had the third highest level of productivity amongst the original 24 OECD countries... Since 1980 only three of the OECD countries have had a worse productivity growth rate than Canada."

Analysts continue to warn of the risks unless R&D spending and innovation are increased. Even David Dodge, former governor of the Bank of Canada, says, "Without a much more innovative economy, we Canadians will not be able to sustain a caring society including universal healthcare." His prediction: "We face the dangers of declining standards of living."[8]

One of the other factors behind our flagging R&D and innovation is foreign ownership. Yet we continue to allow the take-over of our home-grown success stories by wealthy foreign companies. Noted economist Jim Stanford points out that "extensive foreign ownership in Canada undermines innovative activity since most multinationals do their research and development at home near their head office." He adds, "It's clear that there is a failure of Canadian companies to pro-actively embrace innovation as a key business strategy, while contenting themselves instead to raking in the profits from commodities"—with the blessing of the Harper government.[9]

While investment in R&D is key to productivity, investment in human capital is of equally vital importance. Skills training and higher education must be priorities, as must be equality of opportunity and fair compensation. A workforce that sees company profits diverted to enriching those at the top cannot be expected to demonstrate the same loyalty or work ethic as those employed by companies who reward good performance with increased salaries, benefits and bonuses. We simply have to ensure that every Canadian worker feels a vested interest in the development and growth of our national economy.

The government's own procurement of advanced technology can be a significant driver of technological innovation, but according to the WEF, Canada was 48th amongst its member countries in this category.[10] Is it any wonder, when you look at the government's mismanagement of the processes necessary to upgrade our military equipment?

The Harper government's plan to replace aging CF-18 fighter jets with Lockheed Martin's F-35 jets has turned into a saga of unproven technology, questionable delays, disturbing malfunctions, and huge cost overruns. While the government claimed the F-35 fleet purchase—opposed by many Canadians as inappropriate and criticized by both the auditor general and the parliamentary budget officer as ill-planned—would cost $16-$18 billion, the price estimate eventually ballooned to as high as $45 billion.[11]

Another serious obstacle to innovation development in Canada is the Harper government's excessive focus on tar sands oil production and pipelines at the expense of other areas of the economy. Despite all the rhetoric about programs for the benefit of "hard-working Canadians," Harper has presided over a single-commodity oil agenda that benefits primarily big oil companies. As the recent collapse of oil prices has demonstrated all too clearly, this strategy is a mistake no matter what the commodity. It's a recipe for fiscal calamity: even as we are still in recovery from the 2008–11 recession, the economy suffers another blow because so much of its fate is tied to a single resource. The OECD put it politely in 2012: "Canada is blessed with abundant natural resources, but it needs to do more to develop other sectors of the economy if it is to maintain a high-level of employment and equitable distribution of the fruits of growth."

And at a moment when much of the industrialized world is working to reduce its reliance on fossil fuels, where is the investment in technology to find cleaner energy alternatives? This blind pursuit of oil's fortunes reveals a regime that is completely out of touch with national and international realities. It's time for it to go.

— 9 —
MISMANAGEMENT OF THE ECONOMY, PART 2
FEDERAL DEFICIT VOODOO

A GLOBE AND MAIL piece by economist Jim Stanford caught my attention in the summer of 2014: it was a succinct rebuttal of Stephen Harper's inflated spin on his government's fiscal track record. Canadians have been hearing it for four years and they will hear it again, repeatedly, in this election year. Jim wrote:

> Ever since the global meltdown of 2008, it's been an article of faith in Canadian economics that we somehow managed the whole mess better than the rest of the world ... Our recession, while painful, was not nearly as bad as America's. Our deficits were smaller, and will disappear sooner. Not surprisingly, there's a strong political aspect to that smug mindset. Federal Conservatives never tire of claiming credit for this supposedly superior performance.

The argument that Canada outperformed the rest of the world was overstated at the best of times. Even in the early years of recovery several other countries (including Germany, South Korea, Australia) did much better at protecting employment and rebuilding incomes. But with the rest of the world now gaining serious economic momentum, Canada's boastful claims are increasingly far-fetched.[1]

In the run up to the 2015 federal election, the Harper government will try to convince Canadians that the prime minister and his crew have been excellent managers of the Canadian economy and that only they are capable of delivering the same stellar results in the future. Heading into this election, they had intended to present a balanced federal budget as proof of their sound stewardship. But as I write this in spring 2015, the latest projections are that the Harper government will have difficulty delivering the long-promised surplus this year. Thanks to the precipitous fall in oil prices and revenues, the government's budgetary watchdog, Mostafa Askari, estimated a deficit as high as $1.2 billion for this year, and as much as a $400 million the year following.[2]

However, if the government is determined, Askari said, a balanced budget is still feasible should they choose to slow spending or delay capital projects.[3] With the government's earlier forecasts in a tailspin, the budget for the current fiscal year was delayed, no doubt to allow time for a wizard to conjure new numbers that will allow Harper to pull a triumphant, balanced budget out of the proverbial hat.

Magic tricks notwithstanding, the government's fiscal management record hardly warrants applause. Canada's trade position, for example, has been deteriorating steadily. A telling indicator is our current account balance, the broadest measure we have of trade health. It is the sum of the balance of trade (exports minus imports of goods and services) and net investment income (such as interest and dividends). Today we have one of the highest current account *deficits* in the world.

In 2012, in different times, Andrew Hepburn wrote in *Maclean's* that our "export deterioration is, amazingly, worse than it may first appear. Unsurprisingly, data from National Bank shows a sharp rise in the value of Canadian energy exports since 2004 alongside the oil boom (these exports are included in the merchandise trade statistics). At the same time, though, net non-energy exports have plunged from approximately $30 billion in 2000 to about negative $60 billion by 2011. That's a swing of roughly $90 billion... the divergent paths of energy and non-energy exports (aside from other commodities) is startling... It is in this context that Canada has recently experienced a vibrant debate about whether the flourishing of the commodity sector is indeed causing other manufacturers to suffer." And then he asks prophetically, "What happens if resource prices fall significantly from current levels?"[4] The answer to that question is emerging in early 2015 with a hamstrung government and a postponed budget.

The Harper government makes many claims but the numbers don't lie: on a wide range of economic indicators, Canada's performance is declining. Below are a number of statistics and comparisons, many from the OECD Factbook 2014, that provide an overview of our economic status and the overall fiscal health of the country.

- Whereas once Canada was among the world's leading exporters, we're now ranked 28th in exports of goods and services as a percentage of GDP.[5] Canada's share of world exports has been declining for more than a decade. In the eight years before the Harper government took office, Canada had a cumulative trade surplus with other countries of $410 billion. However, during Harper's first nine years in office, that trade surplus fell to a deficit of $56 billion.[6]

- According to the International Monetary Fund, government debt as a percentage of GDP in 2013 put Canada in 13th place amongst the 30 most advanced economies, worse than Austria, the Netherlands, Israel, Germany, Finland, Sweden, Norway, Australia and many others.[7]

- For almost 30 years, Canada enjoyed an average annual GDP growth rate of 2.275 percent, but in 2015 we'll have trouble reaching 2 percent. In dollar terms, that drop represents a huge difference.[8]

- In terms of GDP per capita, Canada ranks 12th amongst OECD countries. All of the following countries have a higher GDP per person income than we do: Luxembourg, Norway, Switzerland, the U.S., Australia, Austria, Ireland, the Netherlands, Sweden, Denmark, and Germany.[9]

- If we look at GDP per hours worked, Canada falls even further to 15th place in the OECD survey, outranked by Norway, Luxembourg, Ireland, the U.S., Belgium, the Netherlands, France, Denmark, Germany, Switzerland, Sweden, Austria, Australia, and well below the G7 average.[10]

- In terms of our employment rates, 11 OECD countries have a higher proportion of persons of working age in employment, and Canada has one of the highest rates of part-time employment in the OECD.[11]

- With respect to hours spent in paid employment on a per capita basis, 16 OECD countries have higher numbers than we do.[12]

- Regarding unemployment figures, 19 OECD countries have lower rates of unemployment in a recent three year average.[13]

- Canada's unemployment rate is higher than it was before the 2008–11 recession. The Canadian Labour Congress pegged the unemployment rate well above the official figure of 7 percent, to 10.8 percent, if involuntary part-time workers and discouraged job seekers were included.[14]

- At the end of 2014, the participation rate in Canada's labour market hit a 13-year low at 66 percent, more than a percentage point below 2008 levels.[15]

- We lag at 14th position in terms of annual growth in compensation per hours worked. All of these countries have seen higher growth in wage rates: Estonia, the Slovak Republic, Hungary, Slovenia, Mexico, Korea, Norway, the Czech Republic, Australia, Poland, Great Britain, Luxembourg, and Denmark.[16]

- In terms of exports of technology, 14 countries export more, measured in millions of dollars, than we do.[17]

- Turning to education: in mathematics, reading and science test scores, Canada is in 7th place; not so long ago, we ranked 3rd.[18]

- Looking at research workers, 14 countries have higher rates per 1000 of full-time researchers.[19] One bright spot is found in the percentage of the population that has attained tertiary (higher or post-secondary) education: we're the 3rd highest in the world, suggesting that individual Canadians continue to excel but in a country that is losing its standing in many other areas. Where will our new graduates find meaningful employment in a nation with sluggish growth and diminished prospects?[20]

- As for social spending, an astonishing 24 OECD countries spend more than Canada as a percentage of GDP, contrary to the claims of our right-wing commentators.[21]

- We have one of the lowest rates of practicing physicians per 1000 inhabitants. Only 11 OECD countries have fewer physicians than Canada, but our total public and private combined expenditures on health are the 6th highest in the world.[22]

- Unbelievably, 28 OECD countries have lower infant mortality rates than Canada.[23]

- Finally, let's look at our total tax revenue as a percentage of GDP. The myth among Chamber of Commerce types and a few pundits is that we're a high-tax, over-taxed country. In fact, 24 OECD countries have a higher percentage of total tax revenue as a percentage of GDP than does Canada.[24]

Far from leading, we now lag behind many other countries on significant economic and social indicators, and our
relative under-performance is only getting worse.

In the next election, the Harper Conservatives will boast
about their role in helping Canada weather the 2008–11
recession, but bear in mind that the strong regulatory frame-
work that helped our financial and banking institutions
maintain stability was not the work of this government, but
rather the result of many decades of strong fiscal governance
by others.

Economist Jim Stanford has made careful comparisons of
Harper's claims against his actual performance in articles for
the *Globe and Mail* and others. Stanford says that there are
some 400,000 discouraged unemployed workers who do
not appear in the official unemployment statistics and that
with other forms of hidden unemployment, the true unemployment rate in recent years is above 12 percent. New job
creation in Canada has barely kept pace with its population
growth; indeed, in 2013 Canada ranked in the lower half of
industrial countries with net job creation lagging 1.4 points
behind population growth.[25]

"When Canadian officials boast that the pace of job-cre-
ation or GDP growth is relatively high," Stanford states, "they
neglect to mention that Canada's economy must generate
more growth and jobs just to stand still... Canada's real
GDP growth since the pre-recession peak (in 2007) ranks an
uninspiring 17th among the 34 countries of the OECD... Real
per capita GDP remains 1.4 percent lower than it was at the
beginning of 2008. In fact, real per capita GDP is still lower
in Canada than it was at the beginning of 2006 (when the

Harper Conservative government first took power); during almost six years of Conservative 'stewardship,' therefore, Canadians have experienced no economic progress (by this measure) whatsoever."[26]

The Canadian economy continues to operate well below its potential with far too many Canadians left behind. During the worst of the recent recession, in 2008 and 2009, Canada experienced the fastest decline in the employment rate of any recession since the 1930s. According to Stanford, we remain mired in a "recession-like funk," still trying to recover from the lingering damage of that catastrophe, while the Harper government pretends otherwise. "The self-congratulatory tone of so many official economic pronouncements in Canada is clearly unjustified."[27]

Saskatchewan MP Ralph Goodale says that the Harper government's growth record is the worst since the days of R.B. Bennett. He says of Harper, "In 2006, he was handed a steadily growing economy which had generated 3.5 million net new jobs, declining debt and taxes, a decade of balanced budgets, annual surpluses at about $13-billion ... That's what Mr. Harper had to work with—the most robust fiscal situation in the western world. And he blew it in less than three years."[28]

Goodale points out that Stephen Harper put the country back into deficit, *"before* (not because of) the recession which arrived in late 2008."[29] And he has delivered six years of budgetary deficits since. He sums up the impact for Canadians, "Since 2006, (the middle-class has) endured nine years of frustrating stagnation, insecure jobs, declining job quality, flat incomes, ballooning debt, escalating education costs, low savings, inadequate pensions and the growing spectre of the current generation of young Canadians not doing as well as their parents did."[30]

Department of Finance Fiscal Reference Tables reveal that in the years before Harper became prime minister, there were nine consecutive years of budgetary surpluses, from 1997 to 2007. In eight of those years, Ottawa amassed a surplus of over $79 billion. But in Harper's first eight years as prime minister, he managed to produce a deficit of almost $127 billion.[31]

From now until the 2015 federal election, we can expect to hear many times from both the prime minister and Finance Minister Joe Oliver how successful they have been taming the deficit and achieving a surplus, some of which they will pass along to taxpayers in tax cuts. But we must ask ourselves, at what price? What programs and services have been slashed or eliminated?

How difficult can it be to balance the books when cuts and closures rule the day and program spending is estimated to have fallen by some $4 billion last year alone? The Harper government has cut almost 26,000 public service jobs in the last three years and, as I've outlined in previous chapters, they have dropped or axed many important programs and services.[32]

Of course we all want balanced books, but balanced by increased economic growth and increased revenue from corporations paying their fair share of taxes, not by draconian measures that hobble our economy, shrink our workforce, and inflict long-term damage on our future prospects. Balancing the books is only meaningful when it has been achieved in concert with strong, healthy social programs and a thriving population with secure employment, accessible healthcare, and affordable homes.

What we are not likely to be reminded of in the Harper government's election year messaging is the accumulated deficit, or national debt, that has grown from almost $482 billion, the year before they came to office, to $612 billion as of March 31, 2014.[33] This represents a massive increase of $130 billion on their watch. Nor will we hear Harper or Oliver talk about the enormous public debt charges that we have had to pay on that national debt during their years in office. Since 2005–06, these charges have exceeded a whopping $280 billion dollars. And that's just to March 31st of 2014.[34]

While the government rhapsodizes about its ability to produce a balanced budget and cut taxes, we will have paid over $28 billion in public debt charges just for the fiscal year ending March 31, 2014 alone.[35] Can you imagine what $28 billion could do to ameliorate child poverty in this country? Or let me put it another way: is this sound economic management?

It wasn't so long ago that Canada was a world leader in policy designed to produce a better, fairer and more just country for everyone. In recent years, all this has changed. Canada has dropped down the list of socially-progressive countries, with levels of poverty that most other major developed countries would not tolerate. Canada is changing rapidly and for the worse.

As readers know, I have spent much of my lifetime sounding the alarm about the damaging impacts of foreign takeovers and so-called free trade on our economic well-being; those issues were explored in great depth in my previous books. Suffice it to say here that while the foreign takeover phenomenon pre-dates the Harper government, it's worth recalling the critical role that it has played, and continues to play, in the hollowing out of our nation. There are ongoing tragic repercussions for our economic well-being, our sovereignty, and our ability to steer our own economy.

While many Canadians are distressed by the loss of iconic Canadian companies like the Hudson's Bay Company and Tim Hortons, the same can't be said of our governments. They have mechanisms at their disposal to stop the wholesale sell-off of our nation but they fail to act. Under Stephen Harper, we have continued to bid good-bye to far too many of our home-grown success stories. How will we ever recover these assets when they are gone?

Here is a partial list of Canadian companies sold to foreigners during a single month in 2014:

- an integrated petroleum company
- a major software design company
- a manufacturer of office and school supplies
- a marine construction services company
- a company that bottles alcoholic beverages
- a company that licenses, markets and distributes alcoholic beverages
- a firm that provides translation services
- a manufacturer and distributor of piano parts, tools and supplies
- a second translation services company
- a company that provides software and information technology
- a company that designs, develops and sells video game engines

- a company that provides solid waste collection, removal and transportation
- a company that explores for and develops mineral resources
- a company that provides wireless cost control management

There is no sign that the Harper government intends to do anything about this sell-off. It will continue, every day of every week of every month.

Along with foreign takeovers, I have long warned Canadians about the downsides of free trade agreements. Like takeovers, free trade agreements erode our sovereignty and undermine Canadian control of our own economy and environment. They allow foreign corporations to sue us for lost profits; in fact, Canada is now the most sued country under NAFTA's free-trade tribunals.[36] The bulk of the lawsuits contest our environmental laws. When listening to Stephen Harper's claims of his government's breakthrough successes in trade negotiations, ask yourself, success for whom?

Maude Barlow and the Council of Canadians have managed to obtain information about the highly secretive trade deal that the government has been negotiating with the European Union—just the latest in a series of agreements reached with countries like Panama, Columbia, Peru, Honduras, Jordan and South Korea.[37] Here is what Maude had to say in a recent letter to Council supporters:

> After five years of secret negotiations that have kept you, me and even parliament in the dark—the proposed Canada-European Union Trade Agreement (or CETA) has just

been leaked. What does this massive trade deal have to do with me, you ask? You'll be shocked.

Your family's health care. Your community's water. Even your right to "buy local." Nothing is off limits in what adds up to the worst corporate sell-out of our country and our rights ever seen. Now we know why he's been hiding it...

Under the deal Canada and European corporations will be given unprecedented rights to challenge barriers to their profit-making—including local, provincial and federal regulations that protect our environment and uphold the public good. And the most dangerous part? Giant corporations like Nestle and Shell will be able to sue Canada for potentially billions in lost profits.

Trade isn't a dirty word. But CETA isn't about trade. Stephen Harper is locking us into a corporate rights deal.

Where you and I and our families stand to be hit hardest is our health care. The cost of pharmaceuticals is pegged to skyrocket by as much as $1.65 billion under the Canada-EU deal. Why? Because Stephen Harper caved to the greed of European drug companies, agreeing to extend patent protections on brand name drugs.

Your city council will no longer be able to favour local businesses. European companies must be given equal consideration to bid on local jobs and contracts. If they aren't, they have the right to file a corporate lawsuit based on discrimination.

The same goes for your right to say "no" to industrial projects in your community. Right now U.S.-based fracking company Lone Pine Resources is using a similar corporate lawsuit provision in NAFTA to sue Canada for $250 million because a Quebec moratorium on fracking is preventing the company from drilling. Imagine your tax dollars paying Big Oil millions to not destroy our environment!

No so-called trade deal is worth all this.[38]

It's yet another agreement that trades away sovereignty and our rights as citizens to make decisions based on our collective needs as a nation and as stewards of the land. Like the Free Trade Agreement and NAFTA before it, and despite overwhelming evidence to the contrary, we'll be told the same breathless fairy tales of its unquestioned benefits.

Please keep all of this in mind during the lead up to the federal election and as you head to the polls later this year. No amount of media or political spin can change the reality that many Canadians across this country are struggling to make ends meet in an economy that is increasingly geared towards rewarding the rich. Canada is drifting towards a state and a condition that is unrecognizable.

We must take back the country and ensure that we protect our citizens and our values. Contrary to what Stephen Harper and his cohorts would have you believe, it is possible to have a thriving economy, a healthy environment, and a compassionate society. In fact, it is the only sustainable way forward.

— 10 —

PROTECTING OUR FUTURE
REFORMING THE ELECTORAL SYSTEM

SINCE MY LAST book, *The Truth About Canada*, was published, I have had many people asking what I think should be our number one priority in improving the country. My answer to this question is the same as it has been for much of the past 30 years: We urgently need electoral reform.

I dealt with this issue at length in *The Truth About Canada*, and I'm repeating some of the material here because the subject has never been more critical than it is today. Unfortunately, as the *Globe and Mail* points out, "Basic though it is, electoral reform is one of those *Important Topics That Cause Eyes to Glaze Over*."[1] But, as Canadians, it is critical that we invest the time and energy necessary to finally correct our dysfunctional electoral system so that we can safeguard our democracy and our future.

Over recent decades, poll after poll has shown that the public has become increasingly disillusioned with politicians and politics, and they have become even more so today. Almost 40 percent of those who did not vote in a recent election said that the elections didn't matter, or they felt they had no one to vote for. In a UN list of 179 countries, when voter turnout was calculated as a percentage of all eligible voters, Canada placed way down in an astonishing 93rd place (the United States was 134th), and in the OECD, we ranked 28th out of 34 countries.

Only a small percentage of Canadians say they trust politicians and feel their votes matter. In one poll, 70 percent said they believed politicians were corrupt. In another poll, the level of trust for politicians was 10%. Among the 30 OECD countries, 18 have a greater proportion of respondents than Canada who say they have a high level of trust in parliament.[2]

Voters have become more and more cynical. But why shouldn't they be, given the shenanigans and corruption and broken promises we've seen in Ottawa during the Mulroney, Chrétien, Martin years, and the abuse of power we've witnessed under Harper?

(Peter C. Newman says that Canadians have become so cynical about politicians that even when Cabinet ministers admit they lied nobody believes them.)[3]

One appalling result of all this is that over 80 percent of adult Canadians have never belonged to a political party, and fewer than 2 percent of adult Canadians make a donation to a political party.[4] In fact, it's worse than that. In the 2011 federal election, less than one percent of eligible voters made a political donation.

How can we begin to change this? I believe we urgently need a mixed-member proportional representation system.

Here are just a few examples of the absurdity of the present system (unless otherwise indicated, the statistics in this chapter have been provided by the excellent organization, Fair Vote Canada):

- In what is perhaps one of the most telling comparisons: in 2008, the Conservatives won a minority government with 37.65% of the vote but, in 2011, they won a "majority" government with 39.62% of the popular vote. A small 1.97% increase in the vote share was enough to hand them 54% of the House of Commons seats and 100% of the power.

- Out of 14 million who showed up to vote, the 2011 majority government was decided by only 6201 votes spread across 14 swing ridings—ridings where the "winner" was decided by a handful of votes.

- In 2011, 7 million voters—about half of all voters, including voters for every party—cast wasted votes—votes which elected no-one.

- In 2011, the federal Conservatives in Alberta received 66% of the vote, but elected 96% of the MPs—27 of 28 seats went to the Conservatives. In Saskatchewan, Conservatives received 56% of the vote, but got 13 out of the 14 seats—92%.

- In the 2008 federal election, the New Democrats received a million more votes than the Bloc, but the Bloc received 49 seats in the House of Commons while the NDP got only 37.

- In 2008, the Green Party received almost a million votes across Canada—close to the number of votes received by the Bloc—yet elected not a single MP, compared to 49 for the Bloc.

With proportional representation, regional representation would be infinitely fairer, votes would count, and results would much better reflect voter intentions.

Larry Gordon of Fair Vote Canada puts this important topic well:

> First-past-the-post has a devastating effect on Canadian unity by exaggerating and exacerbating regional differences. By over-rewarding parties with a strong regional base of support and suppressing... minority political views, the resulting electoral map masks the variety of political views held in all regions. Canadians in all regions have a diversity of views but the electoral map makes Canada look like a hodge-podge of partisan fiefdoms.

Fair Vote Canada (www.fairvote.ca), notes the persistent distortions of winner-take-all voting over the course of decades:

- In almost every federal election since 1980, about half of voters elected no one. In countries using proportional voting systems, almost every vote counts towards electing representation. In NZ in 2011, only 3.4% percent of votes were wasted, 4.9% in Norway (2013) and 1.4% in Sweden (2012).

- Canada ranks a terrible 55th among nations in our percentage of women MPs—behind countries like Rwanda and Mozambique—and 20th out of 34 OECD countries.

- In 2011 it took only 35,152 votes on average to elect a Conservative MP, 43,810 votes to elect an NDP MP, 81,855 to elect a Liberal, 222,857 votes to elect a Bloc, and 572,095 to elect the single Green MP in the House.

- Since World War I, Canada has had 16 "majority" governments. In each case, one party held a majority of seats and exercised almost all of the power. But only 4 of the 16 actually won a majority of the popular vote. Four legitimate majority governments over the past eight decades! The last time a majority of Canadians voted for a single party was in 1984.[5]

Now, let's look at how fair the regional distribution of seats has been in the House of Commons. The answer is not very. As of the 2015 election, Canada will have 30 new federal ridings spread across the country, bringing the total to 338 ridings. The 10 provinces will share a total of 335 ridings and each of the territories will have 1. From the 2011 census, Canada's total population is 33,476,688 of which 33,369,423 live in the 10 provinces, and 107,265 live in the territories.

Based on these figures, by population: Ontario should have 129 ridings but will have only 121; Quebec should have 79 ridings but will have 78; BC should have 44 ridings but will have 42; Alberta should have 37 ridings but will have 34; Manitoba should have 12 ridings but will have 14; Saskatchewan should have 10 ridings but will have 14; Nova Scotia should have 9 ridings but will have 11; New Brunswick should have 8 ridings but will have 10; Newfoundland & Labrador should have 5 ridings but will have 7, and PEI should have one riding but will have 4.

The six small provinces have 15 MPs too many. The four large ones have 14 too few.

Does the unfairness of the system turn people off? One survey said that of the 40 percent of Canadians under 30 years of age, only 5 percent had ever belonged to a political party and the average age of a political party member was 59. Only 3% of party members were between 18 and 25.

Now let's turn to the question of voter turnout.

How do Canadians feel about our democracy and the way it functions? In April 2006, in a Leger Marketing poll, only 36 percent of respondents said that Canada is governed by the will of the people. If this is how people feel, is it any wonder that in recent years voter turnout has been declining? In 1958, 1962 and 1963, it was over 79 percent. In 2008, we hit an all-time low of 58.8%. It rebounded slightly to 61.1% in 2011.

How does this compare with other countries? In 2014, the Conference Board of Canada placed Canada's voter turnout at 14th out of 17 peer countries. In 2011, Canada was 131st in the world for voter turnout, just ahead of Uganda and behind Estonia, while seven other democracies enjoy voter turnout rates in the 80 to 90 percent range.

Of course, aside from our highly unrepresentative voting system, there are other important reasons for low voter turnout, including the corruption, disillusionment and disappointment, and the seemingly perpetual list of broken political promises and the perception (correct for so much of the past) that a wealthy plutocracy's big money has been calling the shots in politics in this country.

106 | THE ARROGANT AUTOCRAT

How about young people, "the future of our country"? Between 70 and 75 percent of 18- to 24-year-old registered voters don't bother to vote. Many young people said they didn't vote because of lack of interest, and 41 percent between the ages of 25 and 34 gave the same answer. Asked to name the most important issue in an upcoming federal election, almost 30 percent said either that there wasn't one or that they didn't know of one. Of the non-voters, 37 percent said either that the elections didn't matter or they didn't like the choices.

All in all, a dismal picture.

In one poll of adult voters, when asked if big business was in charge of our politics because of globalization, 74 percent agreed. When asked if political leaders told the truth and kept their promises, 73 percent said no—the same percentage that said government didn't care about average people. In a March 2005 Leger Marketing poll, when Canadians were asked who, out of a long list, they trusted, they put politicians dead last, at only 14 percent.

The profound impacts of Jean Chrétien's unexpected Bill C-24 which severely limits corporate and trade union political donations (in effect as of January 1, 2004), still remains to be fully recognized in much of the media, and hence by most Canadians. But the new financing rules have had a huge impact on party financing. The Liberals have suddenly found that the "automatic" big-dollar corporate fundraising that they relied on so successfully for so many years is no longer possible.

(Chrétien's completely surprising 2004 political financing legislation was one of only three really important things that he did while prime minister, the others being keeping

Canada out of the Iraq war and the clarity legislation regarding future Quebec referenda.)

That said, all is not perfect. Unlimited secret personal donations are still allowed for leadership and constituency candidates as long as it is prior to acclamation, and while political spending is limited during a federal election there are otherwise no limits. As well, there is a major loophole in the existing legislation which allows an individual to make contributions of $199.99 to every federal riding—a total of more than $60,000—since riding associations are required to notify Elections Canada only when they receive donations of $200 or more. The loophole should be, and easily can be, closed.

In March of 2005, I wrote to my e-mail list:

Canada has moved away from the terrible U.S. system where big corporations and single-issue lobbies ignore funding legislation by channelling enormous amounts of money for politicians through the PACs and the successful re-election rate of incumbents is laughable. If we could combine our own funding legislation with a mixed-member proportional representation system we'll have gone a long way towards making Canada the kind of true democracy most of us want to see.

So, ignore those who suggest we go back to dark-age political financing rules. We've had enough of defence contractors, oil and forestry companies, law firms, accountancy firms, and the wealthy financing politicians with the inevitable results that our tax policies and our social policies fail to reflect the true wishes of our citizens as clearly spelled out, year after year, in poll after poll.

It's time progressive policies not fat bank balances determined political leadership. Do we really want another Paul Martin or for that matter another Brian Mulroney and their big-money friends running the country?

The example of Paul Martin's almost $12 million war chest in the campaign for the Liberal leadership was a perfect example of money from big business and big professional firms warping the democratic process. Martin's millions, mostly from big corporations and their CEOs, made it virtually impossible for anyone else to mount an effective, competitive campaign. For Martin, $5,000-per-person cocktail parties were a norm. In March 2006 in Toronto, 2,000 people attended a Liberal fundraiser. Tables for 10 sold for $8,000. Most tables were purchased by large corporations, and a few by trade unions. The evening netted the Liberal Party $1.4 million.

So, in the past, before the financing reforms, what did it take to make a serious bid for the Liberal leadership? Probably a minimum of $3 million to $5 million, and often much more was spent and not reported. Belinda Stronach is reported to have spent $4 million on her campaign for the leadership of the Conservative Party.

To the total surprise of almost everyone, in 2006 Stephen Harper continued the Chrétien ban on all donations from corporations and trade unions, but also lowered the maximum donation from individuals from $5,000 to only $1,000. As of January 1, 2007, individual Canadians could donate up to a total of an inflation-adjusted $1,100 to each registered political party, and a maximum of an additional $1,100 per year to a registered political association or to contestants for nominations or constituency candidates, whether repre-senting a party or running independently, plus a maximum of $1,100 to a party leadership candidate. This move by Ste-phen Harper astonished many observers. Equally surprising is the fact that Harper hasn't abolished the tough limits on third-party election advertising and election donations, something he vigorously opposed before becoming prime minister.

The *Toronto Star*'s Carol Goar concludes:

No future prime minister will be beholden to corporate interests, as every national leader from Sir John A. Macdon-ald to Paul Martin has been to some degree. Big Business will never be able to mount another massive blitz, as it did in the 1988 election, to promote free trade with the United States. The era of $5,000-a-plate political fundraisers (at least at the federal level) is over.

Because this story has no single hero and no sudden breakthrough, it hasn't made headlines. But from a citizen's point of view, it ranks as one of the most positive—and sur-prising—developments of 21st century politics.

Who would have believed, at the dawn of the millen-nium, that Chrétien, who raked in millions at fundraising dinners, would pull the plug on corporate donations?

Who would have believed the Liberal Party, whose president Stephen LeDrew denounced Chrétien's plan as "dumb as a bag of hammers," would enact the ban?

Who would have believed Broadbent, supported by the autoworkers for 14 years as NDP leader and 21 years as MP for Oshawa, would propose an end to political donations by unions?

Most of all, who would have believed that a political system tainted by the sponsorship scandal, infected by public cynicism and dependent on corporate largesse would be getting cleaner and more transparent by 2007?

There is still work to be done.

An area that needs tidying up is the definition of a political contribution and a campaign expense. As long as big-ticket items such as polling and convention fees lie outside the rules, there will be room for slippage.

On balance, though, Canada has come a long way in a remarkably short time.[6]

By the way, the United States is going in exactly the opposite direction. In a country that already had the most undemocratic big-money-dependent system of election financing, the U.S. Supreme Court in June 2007 further relaxed the ludicrously ineffective regulations relating to corporate and union political spending.

While at the federal level the reforms in political financing have been profound, the prospects for reform of the voting system likely depend on a concerted campaign of strong public pressure. When first elected, the Harper Conservatives promised in a Throne Speech to consider the question of electoral reform. They hired a Winnipeg-based conservative think tank to conduct focus groups. This same think tank had published articles arguing strongly against proportional representation and in favour of the status quo. The exercise was clearly nothing more than a charade.

Like Harper, Jean Chrétien once told reporters he would introduce proportional representation "right after the next election" if he became prime minister. Fair Vote Canada tells what happened: "In 1993, Jean Chrétien wins the election and begins his ten-year reign as prime minister. In three elections, he never wins more than 42 percent of the popular vote, but still forms 'majority' governments thanks to the current voting system. He never gets around to introducing proportional representation."

I've been saying for some 30 years that if we could only get a reformed political financial system that prevented corporations, trade unions and the wealthy from dominating the financing of federal politics, and if we could combine that with a proportional representation electoral system, we'll have gone a very long way down the road to making Canada a much better, fairer, more democratic country.

Well, we're halfway there, and many of us who worked hard for the reform of election financing really didn't believe it would ever happen.

Currently proportional representation exists in over 80 countries including: Argentina, Austria, Belgium, Bolivia, Brazil, Chile, Colombia, the Czech Republic, Denmark, Finland, Germany, Greece, Hungary, Iceland, Indonesia, Ireland, Israel, Italy, Luxembourg, Mexico, the Netherlands, New Zealand, Nicaragua, Norway, Panama, Paraguay, Peru, Poland, Portugal, Serbia, Slovakia, Slovenia, South Africa, Spain, Sweden, Switzerland, Turkey, Uruguay, and Venezuela. Eighty-five percent of OECD countries—our peers—use some form of PR.

If they can do it, surely we can, too!

Pure proportional representation would have the number of those elected as an identical reflection of the percentage of the popular vote received. For example, if party X received 36 percent of the vote in a national or provincial or state election, it would get 36 percent of the seats in the parliamentary chamber.

But some countries have a mixed-member proportional representation system, where the voter casts two votes, one for the constituency candidate they favour, and the other for one of the party lists submitted by the political parties. This system was proposed almost 30 years ago by the Pepin-Robarts commission on national unity, and later, in 2004, by the now defunct Law Commission of Canada after a careful two years of research, consultation, and discussion.

In the MMP system recommended by the Law Commission of Canada, voters also select which individual they would prefer from the party list (this is called the "open list" or "flexible list"), so all MPs are directly elected by voters. Several provinces, including New Brunswick and Quebec, have been encouraged to adopt mixed member proportional (MMP) systems for their legislatures.

To date there have been ten commissions and assemblies in Canada bringing together citizens and experts to look at reforming our electoral system. All have recommended PR. Nine out of ten have recommended MMP.

The Law Commission, in a detailed proposal, suggested that two-thirds of all MPs be elected directly by their constituencies and the balance by proportional representation, using party lists to select the winners, based on the total number of votes received.[7]

There are variations to be considered in a mixed-member proportional system. Germany, New Zealand, Scotland and Wales have 60 percent of the seats reserved for constituency representatives, and 40 percent are selected from party lists. Most countries with a proportional representation system require a minimum of 5 percent of the vote to elect someone to their parliament.

Studies show that countries with proportional representation have higher voter turnouts—7% higher on average. One study suggested that with proportional representation, 1.5 million more Canadians would be casting their vote. Fair Vote Canada reported in 2011 that Canada had far more people not voting at all than voting for the winning party.

Fair Vote Canada says, based on the large number of countries using proportional or fair voting systems over extended periods of time, international experience demonstrates the following benefits over winner-take-all systems:

- Wasted votes and distorted election results are reduced.
- Phoney majority governments are rare.
- Voter turnout tends to be higher.
- Parliaments are more representative of the range of political views and the composition of the electorate (gender, ethnicity, regions).
- 8% more women are elected—almost any country with more than 30% women elected uses a form of PR.
- These countries maintain strong economic performance.
- Citizens tend to be more satisfied with the way democracy works.[8]

I hope Tom Kent was right that "public opinion will before long compel electoral reform." That the NDP has not pushed for proportional representation as a top priority amazes me. This may be changing, the NDP has now committed to implementing PR if elected in the 2015 federal election and we must hold them to it.

Without strong support, proportional representation or other election reform is difficult to achieve. Witness the narrow technical setback in British Columbia in their 2005 referendum on a single transferable vote (STV) system despite majority approval by voters. Note that in B.C. every household received a brochure outlining the STV system. In 2007 in Ontario, no such thing happened.

The electoral reform proposal put before the people of British Columbia in 2005 received majority support in 77 of B.C.'s 79 constituencies but failed because only just under 60 percent (57.7 percent) of voters approved of the proposed change. Some of those who voted against the STV proposal were swayed by the calculation that a seat in the legislature could be won with less than 17 percent of the vote, while many others thought STV was too complex and generally too difficult to understand.

Briefly, let's look at the October 2007 provincial election in Ontario, where the Liberals won two-thirds of the seats in the election with only 42 percent of the vote, *"a resounding victory"* according to some in the press. Meanwhile, 37 percent of voters supported the mixed-member proportional representation (MMP) system recommended by the Ontario Citizens' Assembly, in what the press called *"a resounding defeat."*

What happened? It's not difficult to explain. Many, if not most, didn't understand what they were being asked to vote on. The public education program was totally inadequate. The *Globe and Mail*'s Roy MacGregor put it this way just before the election: "Half of Ontario voters don't know about the proposals. Just ask a few people in a shopping mall. Shrugs. Embarrassment."[9] Larry Gordon of Fair Vote Canada called the public education campaign "pathetically inadequate" but also pointed out that more people voted for MMP than for three of the four major parties. He also pointed out that if there was a vote among those aged 18 to 24, the MMP referendum would have easily exceeded the threshold required for approval.

It's worth mentioning that critics of proportional representation constantly complain that it would result in minority governments. Yet, it's worth repeating that *in all the federal elections going all the way back to 1921, only four times was a majority government elected with a majority of the vote.*

A few words about the Senate. Here, I've long been with the abolitionists. John Baglow, who has been active on the national council of Fair Vote Canada, writes: "Do we really need an Upper House? New Zealand does quite nicely with only one. The Senate is seen by many as a creaky, elitist institution used to reward the political friends of the party in power."[10] This view has been underscored by the plethora of recent spending scandals in the Senate resulting in some criminal charges.

As far back as I can remember, the Senate has been used by the party in power to send out their fundraisers across the country to raise money for party coffers. Witness for example, Mike Duffy and Pamela Wallin.

Let's get rid of the Senate and expand the elected House of Commons. With a new PR system, we're going to need some more members of Parliament to do the system justice. About the dumbest idea I've heard from Stephen Harper is the guaranteed gridlock-inducing election of Senators, a concept fraught with terrible potential problems of conflict, confusion, and rigor mortis.

Yes, I know all about the constitutional problems entailed in abolishing the Senate. So let's have a period of public discussion and debate, and then a national referendum on the subject. I suspect a strong majority of Canadians would approve of abolition. Can one in ten Canadians name a concrete accomplishment of the Senate? As mentioned previously in this book, they produced an excellent report on poverty, but they lack the power to implement the recommendations. And the representation of the Senate is wonky. For example, British Columbia and Alberta have almost a quarter of Canada's population but only 12 seats in the 105-seat Senate. Atlantic Canada has 30 seats with less than a third of the population of B.C. and Alberta.

We urgently need a sustained effort to create a proportional electoral system that makes sense to Canadians, and that works for our country and for democracy. There are clear lessons to be learned from past efforts to reform the system. Canadians need to vote in a national referendum on electoral reform but only *after* an excellent education campaign and an informed debate. The system and the educational materials should be clear and easy to understand with creative efforts to engage the public.

Polls have repeatedly shown that a strong majority of Canadians are in favour of proportional representation—70% in the last national poll in 2013, with another 6% saying it "depends on the system."

Clearly, what is needed is strong political leadership on the issue.

WHAT ABOUT JUSTIN?
WHAT ABOUT TOM?

W ITH THE NEXT federal election looming, time constraints have limited my ability to recount every Conservative scandal or address fully the pervasive damage that I believe Stephen Harper has inflicted on the nation. I have not mentioned the unprecedented disrespect shown by the prime minister to our much-admired chief justice. Nor the relentless efforts to crush the CBC, the national public broadcaster that has given voice to Canadians' shared concerns and aspirations for 75 years. The fact is that in countless arenas, the Harper government's actions have amounted to an unrelenting, hostile attack on the institutions and traditions that were once the pride of Canadians and made us a model for the world.

The most critical message I wish to convey to readers of this book is that we must defeat Stephen Harper and the Conservatives at the polls, and then begin work immediately to reform the dysfunctional electoral system that allowed him to wreak such havoc in nine short years. Harper is not the only prime minister since Confederation to have led a majority government with less than 50 percent of the popular vote. But until now, I don't think we have appreciated just how fortunate we have been that his predecessors possessed a respect and sense of responsibility for our democracy and for the Canadian people they were elected to serve. To ensure that a performance like Harper's never happens again, we must adopt a proportional representation electoral system that will allow Parliament to much better reflect the will of Canadian voters.

In the meantime, what are our options? Just over a year ago, many people were convinced that Justin Trudeau would soon be on his way back to the prime minister's residence at 24 Sussex Drive. At this writing, the last opinion polls show that he still has a very slim lead over Harper and a more substantial one over Tom Mulcair. But Trudeau's approval ratings have been slipping, as one egregious gaffe after another diminishes voters' confidence. Witness his use of a phallic metaphor regarding military action against the Islamic State or his comments about admiring the kind of government the Chinese Communists have in Beijing.

More troubling is his position on oil pipelines. It's impossible to be in favour of the Keystone XL pipeline, which Trudeau is, and at the same time be serious about tackling climate change. Contradictions of this kind confuse the message. Although we know that Trudeau has assembled a highly talented policy taskforce to help him develop his positions on key issues, the influence of this group of advisors has yet to be discerned. Surely they have been doing more in the past year than studying marijuana legislation around the world, or trying to figure out what to do with the Liberal senators expelled from the caucus. In any event, the election is just a few months away. Trudeau must work with his advisors and pay attention to their advice. Important new policy options from the Liberals are long overdue.

What should Liberal policies look like? First they should be good for the Canadian people as a whole, with social and economic programs that will allow all citizens to participate fully in the future of their country. Second, they must be clearly distinguishable from those of Harper and the Conservatives.

Some examples. Harper's handling of the climate change file is rightly seen as disastrous by many in Canada and around the world. Trudeau has everything to gain and little to lose by getting out in front on global warming and blasting Harper's record in the strongest terms at every opportunity. Science supports the need for strong action and so do most Canadians. Why not get on with it?

Trudeau's recent announcement of a national carbon pricing plan to help cut greenhouse gas emissions was a good beginning, but he proposed that the provinces and territories be allowed to design their own systems. Instead of a cohesive national plan, we could be left with good intentions that are in fact ineffective. Since a major contributor to Canada's greenhouse gas production is the tar sands, do we really want to leave the execution of a carbon tax in the hands of the Alberta government? At the same time, Trudeau undermines his commitment with continuing support for oil pipelines and growth in the tar sands industry.

Next, what about action on the issue of poverty and child poverty in particular? Why not put the Senate's comprehensive report on poverty in front of Stephen Harper and the public every day? The Conservatives' record is truly shameful.

In January of this year, Oxfam International released a report on global wealth inequity that made headlines everywhere. It predicted that by 2016, the world's richest 1 percent will own more of the world's wealth than the remaining 99 percent combined. Oxfam called for a clamp-down on tax dodging by corporations and individuals; the introduction of minimum wages and a living wage for all workers; equal pay legislation, and a fairer sharing of the tax burden. The organization's figures show that the wealth of just 80 individuals now exceeds that of the poorest half of all humans on earth combined. The world's poorest 3.5 billion own less wealth than the richest 80! We can see this reflected here at home where 50 percent of our population earns $30,000 a year or less. Shocking wealth disparity is a Canadian crisis too, one that demands bold leadership; so far, Trudeau has not stepped up on this issue. Why not?

He does have youth, real presence, and a fresh energy on his side. He is attracting attention from a younger generation that many of us worried had turned away from political engagement. And he has a legacy which so far he has worn lightly and to his advantage. I knew Pierre Elliott Trudeau during the heady days of Trudeau-mania, and we worked together on some important issues while I was briefly an adviser on foreign affairs for the Liberal Party, mostly relating to foreign ownership and control. Certainly, Pierre

Trudeau was one of the most interesting men I've ever met, charismatic and undeniably intelligent.

There is no doubt that Justin Trudeau will grow into a stronger and more capable leader, but the question is when? Once the actual election campaign begins, and especially during the televised debates, he'll have to be confident in his positions, cool and reasoned under pressure, and clear on his alternatives to the Harper agenda. He'll also have to withstand the onslaught of Conservative attack ads that could be even more vicious than those that demolished Michael "Just Visiting" Ignatieff.

Tom Mulcair has unquestionably out-performed both Trudeau and Harper in this pre-election period. Mulcair has been forceful, policy-oriented, and articulate, challenging Harper's evasive obscurity on a range of critical issues. He has pushed for essential initiatives like a national daycare program, a social good that we should have put in place twenty years ago. Accessible and affordable daycare would offer single parents and lower and middle-income earners a real opportunity to improve their employment prospects, their standard of living, and their quality of life. Instead, we have a government that abandoned the idea in favour of a smoke-and-mirrors cheque-in-the mail scheme.

Mulcair's promise of a proper minimum wage for workers in federally-regulated sectors such as airports and telecommunications would help the country break out of a wage stagnation that has hobbled the labour market in recent years. Mulcair admits that the number of workers affected initially might be relatively small, but it would put pressure on the provinces and the private sector to follow suit.

Although I have never been a member of the NDP, I have contributed financially to some federal NDP candidates. Linda McQuaig of Toronto, Erin Weir in Saskatchewan, and Michael Byers in Vancouver would make outstanding members of Parliament. I've also been a life-long admirer of Tommy Douglas and published a biography of him in 1987 (*The Road to Jerusalem* by Thomas McLeod). I was fortunate enough to appear on stage with Tommy several times, mostly at events relating to petroleum and pipelines. He was easily the greatest speaker I've ever heard, and he well deserved the title of the "Greatest Canadian of all time," bestowed on him by Canadians in a popular CBC television poll.

I knew Jack Layton very well too and admired him enormously. Inspiring, principled, and compassionate, he is greatly missed still. Mulcair had a tough act to follow. His performance has been solid, with few exceptions, but he has somehow failed to inspire and captivate the imagination of most Canadians.

In the absence of a sure winner to defeat Stephen Harper, many people have urged me to speak out in favour of a centre-left coalition to contest the next federal election. Invariably, they are people who are greatly concerned about Canada's future, but most of them do not fully comprehend how our federal political parties operate. Unfortunately, few Liberal or NDP candidates would be likely to give up their own political aspirations and step aside to cede their constituencies to candidates from another party. It's highly improbable their leaders would agree to a coalition in advance of taking their chances at the polls.

However, this does not mean that a coalition isn't possible. It will depend on the outcome of the election itself. Under the right circumstances, there could very well be a coalition soon after the election, and a powerful coalition at that.

Should the contending parties fail to unseat Stephen Harper in the next federal election, we should urge them to form a coalition for the sake of restoring our democracy and indeed, our civil society.

Each of the three opposition parties and their leaders— Justin Trudeau, Thomas Mulcair and Elizabeth May—have excellent qualities to bring to the table. May has the knowledge and expertise to ensure that every piece of legislation and new policy is measured against the imperative to address climate change, in my opinion easily the most pressing issue that confronts us today.

Consider this scenario. If (God forbid), Stephen Harper wins a minority of seats in the House of Commons—more than the Liberals or the NDP separately, but fewer than the two (or three) parties combined—he will then go to the Governor-General with the expectation of being asked to form the next government. Harper will then convene the next session of Parliament, followed by a throne speech. If the other parties then vote against Harper on a non-confidence motion, it would open the doors for a coalition.

The idea of a coalition of two or more parties is not unprecedented. Following the October 2008 election, the Liberals and New Democrats reached an agreement to form a minority coalition government with support from the Bloc Québécois and the Greens, but the non-confidence vote and coalition never came to fruition due to Harper's prorogation of parliament, and strong opposition from many Canadians to the inclusion of the Bloc.

Obviously if Trudeau and Mulcair are smart, they will enter into their own private agreement to share power and they will also share Cabinet appointments. Such an agreement could last for one, two, or even three years, and once whoever is acting as prime minister is defeated in the House, the Governor General will be sure to call a new federal election.

Earlier this year, Stephen Lewis, former Canadian ambassador to the United Nations and Special UN Envoy on Aids, delivered the 2014 Symons Lecture in Charlottetown, PEI, at the centre commemorating the Fathers of Confederation who had met there almost 150 years before. These words are from the conclusion of his very moving address:

> What in the world is happening to this country... It amounts to the slow, inexorable whittling away at democratic norms. And there is no shame. No shame whatsoever. There is a radical ideological agenda gripping this country, but it's not the environmentalists or the other targeted groups committed to the quest for social justice; it's the political leadership.

The Canada we know and love will not survive another four years of Stephen Harper and his Conservative government. Everything we value is at stake. Let's make sure, with a chorus too loud to ignore, that we demand that Trudeau and Mulcair put Canada first and work together to stop Stephen Harper's takeover and restore democracy to this country.

GLOSSARY

CAMPAIGN 2000 a non-partisan, cross-Canada coalition of over 120 national, provincial and community organizations committed to working together to end child and family poverty in Canada.

CANADA 2020 an independent, progressive think-tank with a mission "to inform and influence debate, to identify progressive policy solutions and to help redefine the federal government for a modern Canada."

CCPA Canadian Centre for Policy Alternatives. This is an independent research institute concerned with issues of social and economic justice. Founded in 1980, the CCPA is one of Canada's leading progressive voices in public policy debates. The CCPA is a registered, non-profit organization supported by more than 10,000 members across Canada, with a national office in Ottawa and provincial offices in Nova Scotia, Ontario, Manitoba, Saskatchewan and British Columbia.

FAIR VOTE CANADA Fair Vote Canada is a grassroots multi-partisan citizens' campaign which works to educate and promote electoral reform and the introduction of proportional representation in Canada.

GDP Gross Domestic Product. The total output of goods and services for final use produced by both residents and non-residents in an economy. This is the standard measure of the incomes generated from productive activity in a country.

INNOVATION The Conference Board of Canada defines economic innovation as "the process through which economic and social value is extracted from knowledge through the generation, development, and implementation of ideas to produce new or improved strategies, capabilities, products, services, or processes."

LAW COMMISSION OF CANADA The Law Reform Commission of Canada was formed in 1971 as a permanent independent body to study and undertake a systematic review of Canadian law. It was shut down in 1993 by former Prime Minister Brian Mulroney and then formed again in 1997, this time as the Law Commission of Canada (LCC). Its mandate was to study and review the laws of Canada and offer independent advice on improvements, modernization and reform aimed at a just legal system that meets the changing needs of Canadian society. It advised Parliament for nine years until its budget was axed in 2006 by Stephen Harper.

LOW INCOME Low income is broadly defined by Statistics Canada as a family or individual income that is half or less of median income.

NATIONAL COUNCIL OF WELFARE (NCW) Formed in 1969, the National Council of Welfare provided welfare and poverty statistics, fact-based social policy resources and served as an advisory group to the federal Minister responsible for the welfare of Canadians. In 2012, the entire $1 million budget of the NCW was eliminated in a single-line item in one of Stephen Harper's omnibus bills.

OECD Organization for Economic Cooperation and Development. This is composed of 34 developed countries which work together on economic, social, globalization and environmental matters. The OECD publishes a steady stream of invaluable books, papers, articles, and studies. The OECD member countries are Australia, Austria, Belgium, Canada, Chile, the Czech Republic, Denmark, Estonia, Finland, France, Germany, Greece, Hungary, Iceland, Ireland, Israel, Italy, Japan, Korea, Luxembourg, Mexico, the Netherlands, New Zealand, Norway, Poland, Portugal, the Slovak Republic, Slovenia, Spain, Sweden, Switzerland, Turkey, the United Kingdom and the United States.

PMO Prime Minister's Office

PRODUCTIVITY (or Labour Productivity)—measures the economic growth of a country. It measures the amount of goods and services produced by one hour of labor or the amount of real GDP produced by an hour of labor. Labor productivity depends on three main factors: investment, new technology and human capital.

PR Proportional Representation—an electoral system in which parties gain seats in proportion to the number of votes cast for them.

NOTES

CHAPTER 1

1 Rathgeber, Brent, *Irresponsible Government: The Decline of Parliamentary Democracy in Canada*, Point of View Books, 2014

2 "Stephen Harper is muzzling Tory MPs and Parliament is diminished," *Toronto Star* editorial, March 29, 2013

3 Martin, Lawrence, *Harperland*, Viking Canada, 2010

4 Cheadle, Bruce, "Tories rebrand *Government of Canada* as *Harper Government*," *Toronto Star*, March 3, 2011

5 CBC News, "A Rebranding of the *Harper Government*," March 4, 2011

6 National Energy Board Website—Applying to Participate in a Hearing, https://www.neb-one.gc.ca/prtcptn/hrng/pplngprtcpt-eng.html

7 Beltrame, Julian, "Budget watchdog takes Harper government to court over information request," *Globe and Mail*, November 21, 2012

8 Chase, Steven, "Federal budget watchdog Kevin Page goes out fighting," *Globe and Mail*, March 22, 2013

9 Berthiaume, Lee, "Government won't share winning shipbuilding bids with budget officer," *Postmedia News*, December 6, 2012

10 "Stephen Harper's war on transparency," *Toronto Star* Editorial, March 11, 2013

11 "Tories kill access to information database," *CBC News*, May 2, 2008

12 Delacourt, Susan, "Dictating the terms of the political conversations," *Toronto Star*, July 20, 2012

13 English, Kathy, "Stephen Harper government builds stone wall around information: Public editor," *Toronto Star*, October 19, 2012

14 Beeby, Dean, "Canada Freedom of Information Ranking Disputed By Harper Government," *Canadian Press*, April 26, 2013

15 Yalnizyan, Armine, "Harper's Attack on Democracy, Itemized by Lawrence

Martin," *Behind the Numbers*, A Blog by the CCPA at behindthenumbers.ca, April 27th 2011

16 Blanchfield, Mike ande Jim Bronskill, "Documents expose Harper's obsession with control," *Canadian Press*, June 6, 2010

17 May, Elizabeth, "The Third Prorogation and why it's not the offence of the earlier prorogations," *Island Tides*, August 28, 2013

18 "Harper's new omnibus budget bill a stealth blow to civil servants," *Toronto Star* Editorial, October 23, 2013

19 Hansard, March 25, 1994

20 Mendes, Errol, "In praise of Stephen Harper, the opposition MP who fought omnibus bills," *Globe and Mail*, November 26, 2012

21 Ibid.

22 Martin, Lawrence, *Harperland*, Viking Canada, 2010, p. 97

23 Travers, Jim, "An eloquent plea for democracy," *Toronto Star*, March 4, 2011

24 Travers, Jim, "The quiet unravelling of Canadian democracy," *Toronto Star*, April 4, 2009

25 Martin, Lawrence, *Harperland*, Viking Canada, 2010, p. 3

26 Ibid.

27 Ibid.

28 "Michael Sona guilty in robocalls trial—*but did not likely act alone*, CBC News, August 14, 2014

29 "Fair Elections Act: Activists Plan Court Challenge to 'Anti-Democratic' Law," *Canadian Press*, September 12, 2014

30 "Poor planning led to unlawful arrests and Charter violations at Toronto G20 summit," *Toronto Star* Editorial, May 16, 2012 and "Police chief to hold officers accountable for G20 conduct," *CTV News* Staff, May 16, 2012

31 Stryker, Alyssa and Carmen Cheung, "Six Things Protesters Need to Know about Bill C-51," *TheTyee.ca*, March 11, 2015

32 "Open letter to Parliament: Amend C-51 or kill it," *National Post*, February 27, 2015

33 "CSIS oversight urged by ex-PMs as Conservatives rush Bill C-51 debate," *CBC News*, February 19, 2015

CHAPTER 2

1 Connor, Steve, "Billionaires secretly fund attacks on climate science," *The Independent*, UK January 24, 2013

2 Ibid.

3 McGrath, Matt, "Climate impacts 'overwhelming'—UN," *BBC News*—Science and Environment, March 31, 2014

4 Bailey, Ian and Alexandra Posadzki, "Forest fires rage across B.C., forcing thousands to flee," *Globe and Mail*, July 18, 2014

5 "Roads resembled rivers in Kamloops flash flood," *Globe and Mail*, July 24, 2014

6 "NWT fires: Gameti, Wekweeti not in immediate danger," CBC *News*, July 10th, 2014

7 Graham, Jennifer, "Flooding forces more Saskatchewan communities to declare emergencies, *Global News*, July 1st, 2014

8 "Tornado tears through Angus, Ont., damaging homes: State of emergency declared in central Ontario township, thousands without power around province," CBC *News*, June 17th, 2014

9 *National Post* Staff and Jake Edmiston, "Catastrophic ice storm slams into Toronto, strands travellers across the province," *Canadian Press*, December 23, 2013 and David Shum, "Delays continue after ground stop lifted at Toronto's Pearson airport," *Global News*, January 7, 2014

10 "Alberta flood recovery could take 10 years, says premier," CBC *News*, June 24, 2013

11 McGrath, Matt, "Climate impacts 'overwhelming'—UN," BBC *News*—Science & Environment, March 31, 2014

12 McGrath, Matt, "Climate inaction catastrophic—US," BBC *News*—Science & Environment, March 31, 2014

13 May, Elizabeth, "Bill C-38: The Environmental Destruction Act," *The Tyee.ca*, May 10, 2012

14 Ibid.

15 Ditchburn, Jennifer, "Conservatives distance themselves from Northern Gateway pipeline decision as NDP, Liberals find a wedge issue," *National Post*, June 18, 2014

16 Clark, Campbell, "Harper's 'yes' to Gateway a big risk in B.C.," *Globe and Mail*, June 17, 2014

17 Simpson, Jeffrey, "The numbers say it all: Canada is a climate-change miscreant," *Globe and Mail*, June 4, 2010

18 Jaccard, Mark, "The Accidental Activist," *Walrus Magazine*, March, 2013

19 McMartin, Pete, "Global warming's frightening new deadline," *Vancouver Sun*, March 9, 2013

20 Jaccard, Mark, "The Accidental Activist," *Walrus Magazine*, March, 2013

21 McMartin, Pete, "Global warming's frightening new deadline," *Vancouver Sun*, March 9, 2013

22 Friedman, Thomas, L., "Obama on Obama on Climate," *New York Times*, June 7, 2014

23 Text of Harper's Speech to the Council for National Policy, June, 1997, CBC *News*—Canada Votes 2006, http://www.cbc.ca/canadavotes2006/leadersparties/harper_speech.html

24 Jaccard, Mark, "Canadians deserve honest climate talk," *Globe and Mail*, August 5, 2014

25 Harris, Sophia, "$24 million ad campaign for Keystone pipeline had little impact: survey," CBC *News*, August 21, 2014

26 "Former Harper advisor blasts Keystone XL support," *Canadian Press*, December 2, 2013

27 Biello, David, "How Much Will Tar Sands Oil Add to Global Warming? To constrain climate change, such unconventional oil use needs to be stopped, according to scientists;" *Scientific American*, January 23, 2013

28 "The Enbridge Northern Gateway Oil Supertanker and Pipeline Project: So much that's precious... too much to risk," A Factsheet from Westcoast Environmental Law, http://wcel.org/pipelines-and-tankers-publications

29 Davison, Janet, "Pipeline push-back: What's behind the rising opposition to Canada's big oil pipelines? Climate change debate behind animosity behind Northern Gateway and Keystone XL," CBC *News*, April 30, 2014

30 Pagliaro, Jennifer, "Natural Resources Minister Joe Oliver says oil opponents haven't asked for meeting," *Toronto Star*, January 27, 2012

CHAPTER 3

1 MacIntyre, Linden, "Silence of the Labs," a Fifth Estate Documentary, CBC, September 11, 2014 http://www.cbc.ca/player/Shows/Shows/the+fifth+estate/ID/2429411271/

2 Turner, Chris, *The War on Science*, Greystone Books, 2013

3 Galloway, Gloria, "Scientists feel muzzled by Conservative government, union says," *Globe and Mail*, October 21, 2013

4 Gatehouse, Jonathan, "When science goes silent: With the muzzling of scientists, Harper's obsession with controlling the message verges on the Orwellian," *Maclean's Magazine*, May 3, 2013

5 Allen, Kate, "*Muzzling* of Canadians scientists sent before Information Commissioner Suzanne Legault," *Toronto Star*, March 15, 2013

6 Semeniuk, Ivan, "Scientists push campaign for evidence-based decision making from government," *Globe and Mail*, September 16, 2013

7 Homer-Dixon, Thomas, Heather Douglas and Lucie Edwards, "Fix the link where science and policy meet," *Globe and Mail*, June 23, 2014

8 Munro, Margaret, "Information commissioner to investigate Harper government's muzzling' of federal scientists," *National Post*, April 1, 2013

9   "Ottawa axes ocean pollution monitoring program," *Vancouver Sun,* May 22, 2012

10 Orihel, Diane and David Shindler, "Experimental Lakes Area is saved but it's a bittersweet victory for science," *Globe and Mail,* April 1, 2014 and, "Experimental Lakes Area research station officially saved: unique research station in northwestern Ontario to be funded by province and non-profit group," CBC News, April 1, 2014

11 "High Arctic research station saved by new funding: Eureka's PEARL gets $5M over 5 years," *CBC News,* May 17, 2013

12 Farewell to the National Roundtable on the Environment and the Economy, the Broadbent Blog, June 13, 2013

13 Chung, Emily, "Foreign scientists call on Stephen Harper to restore science funding, freedom: open letter warns about effects of Canadian science policy on international collaboration," *CBC News,* October 23, 2014

14 Allen, Kate, "*Muzzling* of Canadians scientists sent before Information Commissioner Suzanne Legault," *Toronto Star,* March 15, 2013

15 Ibid.

16 Press Freedom Index, 2013—http://en.rsf.org/press-freedom-index-2013, 1054.html

17 Nikiforuk, Andrew, "What's Driving the Chaotic Dismantling of Canada's Science Libraries? Scientists reject Harper gov't claims vital material is being saved," *TheTyee.ca,* December 23, 2013

18 Nifkiforuk, Andrew, "Dismantling of Fishery Library 'Like a Book Burning' Say Scientists," *TheTyee.ca,* December 9, 2013

19 Paris, Max, "Fisheries and Oceans library closings called loss to science: Fisheries and Oceans plans to close 7 of its 11 libraries across the country," *CBC News,* January 6, 2014

20 Bourrie, Mark, "The War on Brains," *Toronto Star,* January 26, 2015

21 "Health Canada Library Changes Leave Scientists Scrambling," *CBC News,* January 20, 2014

22 Nikiforuk, Andrew, "What's Driving the Chaotic Dismantling of Canada's Science Libraries? Scientists reject Harper gov't claims vital material is being saved," *TheTyee.ca,* December 23, 2013

23 McDonald, Marci, *The Armageddon Factor: The Rise of Christian Nationalism in Canada,* Vintage Canada, 2010

24 Simpson, Jeffrey, "Don't forget the Base, you can bet Harper won't," *Globe and Mail,* June 8, 2013

CHAPTER 4

1   O'Neil, Peter, "The people behind ethical oil," *Vancouver Sun*, August 10, 2012

2   Ryckewaert, Laura, "Where's Velshi, there's PMO influence," *The Hill Times*, March 5, 2012

3   http://www.ethicaloil.org/

4   Proussalidas, Daniel, "Greenpeace: Ethicaloil.org a front for the Tories," *Toronto Sun*, April 8, 2014

5   "Study cites 'chill' from tax agency audits of charities' political activities," *Canadian Press*, July 10, 2014

6   Beeby, Dean, "Timeline of Canada Revenue Agency's political-activity audits of Canadian charities," *Canadian Press*, July, 2014

7   Ibid.

8   Beeby, Dean, " Canada Revenue Agency's political-activity audits of charities," *Canadian Press* / CBC *News*, August 5, 2014

9   Ibid.

10 Beeby, Dean, "CRA audited left-wing think-tank because its research shows 'bias'," *Canadian Press* / *Global News*, September 1, 2014

11 Ibid.

12 "An Open Letter from Dr. David Suzuki,", April 12, 2012

13 "Environmental charities 'laundering' foreign funds, Kent says," CBC *News*, May 1, 2012

14 http://voices-voix.ca/en/facts/profile/physicians-global-survival

15 Beeby, Dean, "CRA accused of 'political' targeting of charities: Charities in first wave of CRA audits were largely opponents of Conservatives' energy policies," *Macleans Magazine*, August 3, 2014

16 Beeby, Dean, "Tax agency says 'preventing poverty' not allowed as goal for charity," *Canadian Press* / *Toronto Star*, July 24, 2014

17 "PEN Canada hit with political-activities tax audit," CBC *News*, July 21, 2014

18 http://pencanada.ca/

19 CRA smacks PEN Canada with audit in latest of Harper government's attack on charities," *Vancouver Observer*, July 22, 2014

20 Beeby, Dean, "PEN Canada hit with political-activities audit by Canada Revenue Agency," *Canadian Press* / *Globe and Mail*, July 21, 2014

21 Beeby, Dean, "Revenue Canada targets birdwatchers for political activity," CBC *News*, October 16, 2014

22 Berthiaume, Lee, "The Canadian International Development Agency is gone," *Postmedia News*, June 27, 2013

23 "Canadian Council for International Cooperation: What Happened," Voices—http://voices-voix.ca/en/facts/profile/canadian-council-international-co-operation

24 Martin, Paul, Joe Clark, Ed Broadbent and Joseph Ingram, "North-South Institute: We've lost a Canadian asset," *Globe and Mail*, September 22, 2014

25 Ibid.

26 Porter, Catherine, "Canada's cut to foreign aid biggest of any country in 2013," *Toronto Star*, October 7, 2014

CHAPTER 5

1 Eggleton, Art, "Three ways to end poverty in Canada," *Toronto Star*, January 5, 2015

2 Kerstetter, Steve, "Scrapping the welfare council is a cheap shot by a government that doesn't care about the poor," *Toronto Star* Editorial Opinion, April 8, 2012

3 Ibid.

4 Sheikh, Munir, "Canada has lost its census anchor," *Globe and Mail*, May 9, 2013

5 Freeman, Sunny, "National Household Survey That Replaced Long-Form Census Is Unreliable: Experts," *Huffington Post*, May 6, 2013

6 Day, Jim, "Ottawa needs to repair damage to census-gathering process: Ivan Fellegi," *The Guardian*, November 8, 2011

7 Yalnizyan, Armine, "National Household Survey provides blurred look at housing," *Globe and Mail*, September 12, 2013

8 "It's a false economy to cut Statscan's budget," Editorial, *Globe and Mail*, April 22, 2014

9 Macdonald, David, "The Fog Finally Clears: The Job and Services Impact of Federal Austerity," *Behind the Numbers*, April 2013

10 "It's a false economy to cut Statscan's budget," Editorial, *Globe and Mail*, April 22, 2014

11 Duffy, Andrew, "The State of StatsCan Survey," *Ottawa Citizen*, August 30, 2014

12 "It's a false economy to cut Statscan's budget," Editorial, *Globe and Mail*, April 22, 2014

13 "Statistics Canada says 34 programs hit by budget cuts," *Reuters*, June 29, 2012

14 Woods, Michael, "Statistics Canada facing more funding cuts, estimates show," *PostMedia News*, February 28, 2013

15 Tarran, Brian, "Canada's Chief Statistician resigns in protest at government plans for census," *Research*, July 23, 2010

16 "89-year-old peace activist acquitted despite refusing to complete census," *Globe and Mail*, October 9, 2013

17 Grant, Tavia, "Damage from cancelled census as bad as feared, researchers say," *Globe and Mail*, January 29, 2015

18 Grant, Tavia, "Canadian income data 'is garbage' without census, experts say," *Globe and Mail*, October 4, 2013

19 Ibid.

20 Armine Yalnizyan is a Senior Economist at the Canadian Centre for Policy Alternatives. This material is taken from emailed material she sent to me in the summer of 2014.

21 Parkinson, David, "Canada is roaming blind through a statistical desert," *Globe and Mail*, April 4, 2014

22 Ibid.

23 "City planning difficult without long-form census data, says Urban Futures Institute," CBC's *On the Coast*, February 6, 2015

24 Notes from Ken Battle, President of the Caledon Institute of Social Policy in Ottawa, June of 2014.

CHAPTER 6

1 UNICEF Canada: *Report Card 10 Measuring Child Poverty* (2012); *Report Card 11 Stuck in the Middle: Child Well-Being in Rich Countries, Canadian Companion* (2013); *Report Card 12 Children of the Recession, Canadian Companion* (2014). www.unicef.ca

2 OECD Factbook 2014, p. 66

3 "Needed: A Federal Action Plan to Eradicate Child and Family Poverty in Canada," *2012 Report Card on Child and Family Poverty*, Campaign 2000, 2012

4 "In From the Margins: A Call to Action on Poverty, Housing and Homelessness," The Standing Senate Committee on Social Affairs, Science and Technology, December, 2009.

5 Ibid.

6 Ibid.

7 "In From The Margins: A Call To Action On Poverty, Housing and Homelessness," The Standing Senate Committee on Social Affairs, Science and Technology, December, 2009.

8 Ogrodnik, Irene, "25 years since Canada vowed to end child poverty, where are we now?" *Global News*, November 23, 2014

9 Harper, Tim, "A bill meant to sow conflict, confrontation with First Nations does its job: Tim Harper," *Toronto Star*, December 9, 2014

10   Klein, Seth and Armine Yalnizyan, "Creating a Just Society: Reducing poverty, inequality will spur economic recovery," March 1, 2010

11   "Needed: A Federal Action Plan to Eradicate Child and Family Poverty in Canada," 2012 Report Card on Child and Family Poverty, Campaign 2000, 2012

12   "Canada's food banks are booming, to our shame: Editorial," *Toronto Star*, November 7th, 2014

13   "Costs keep one third of Canadian children from participating in organized sports," *Newswire*, July 10, 2014

14   Broadbent, Ed, "Canada has failed to create equality of opportunity," *Globe and Mail*, November 24, 2014

15   Shapcott, Michael, "Latest CMHC numbers confirm federal housing cuts will grow deeper as housing needs grow," The Wellesley Institute, June 5, 2012

16   Tucker, Erika and Vassy Kapelos, "Fears of evictions across Canada as feds end co-op housing subsidy," *Global News*, January 22, 2014

17   Curry, Bill, "Everything you need to know about income-splitting," *Globe and Mail*, October 21, 2014

18   "The Dollars and Sense of Solving Poverty," National Council of Welfare Reports, Autumn, 2011

19   "Fighting poverty pays off, report says," *Canadian Press*, September 28, 2011

20   Fine, Sean, "Ottawa's Refugee Health Cuts 'cruel and unusual,'" *Globe and Mail*, July 4, 2014

21   "Response from Minister on refugee transport loans," Canadian Council for Refugees, http://ccrweb.ca/en/response-minister-refugee-transporta-tion-loans (December 15, 2014)

22   "Tories strike another blow to Canada's once-humane immigration policy," *Toronto Star* Editorial, August 4, 2014

23   Contenta, Sandro, "Benhmuda family can return to Canada—if they pay $6,000 it cost to deport them," *Toronto Star*, October 24, 2013

24   Kahane, Adam, "Alex Himelfarb on austerity, inequality, and *trickle-down meanness*," *Globe and Mail*, December 19, 2014

CHAPTER 7

1   McFarland, Janet, "Canada's poor took big financial hit in recent years, report finds," *Globe and Mail*, September 11, 2014

2   The Wealth Gap: Perceptions and Misconception in Canada, The Broadbent Institute, December, 2014

3   McFarland, Janet, "Canada's poor took big financial hit in recent years, report finds," *Globe and Mail*, September 11, 2014

4   Macdonald, David, "Outrageous Fortune: Documenting Canada's Wealth
    Gap," Canadian Centre for Policy Alternatives, April 3, 2014

5   Yalnizyan, Armine, "Study of Income Inequality in Canada: What Can Be
    Done," Presentation to the House of Commons Standing Committee on
    Finance, CCPA, April 30, 2013

6   "Income Inequality," Conference Board of Canada, http://www.conference-
    board.ca/hcp/details/society/income-inequality.aspx (March 2015)

7   "The Case For Leaning Against Income Inequality," Special Report, TD Eco-
    nomics, November 24, 2014

8   "The Canada We Want in 2020: Reducing Income Disparity and Polarization,"
    Canada 2020, November 2011

9   Raphael, Dennis and Toba Bryant, "Income inequality is killing thousands of
    Canadians every year," *Toronto Star*, November 23, 2014

10 "What Did Corporate Tax Cuts Deliver?" Background Report for Corporate
    Tax Freedom Day, Canadian Labour Congress, 2012

11 Ibid.

12 Whittington, Les and Bruce Campion-Smith, "EI Reform: Unemployed
    Canadians face crackdown under federal changes," *Toronto Star*, May 24, 2012

13 "CLC Analysis of the 2013 Federal Budget," Canadian Labour Congress,
    March 21, 2013

14 Grant, Tavia, "The 15-hour work week: Canada's part-time problem," *Globe
    and Mail*, October 4, 2014

15 "The Canada We Want—Reducing Income Disparity and Polarization," Can-
    ada 2020, November 2011

16 Yalnizyan, Armine, "A Problem for Everyone," *National Post*, September 21,
    2011

CHAPTER 8

1   Parkinson, David, "Canada slips a notch in competitiveness ranking," *Globe
    and Mail*, September 3, 2014

2   Semeniuk, Ivan, "Canada losing ground in global science race: report," *Globe
    and Mail*, May 22, 2013

3   OECD (2012), *OECD Economic Surveys: Canada 2012*, OECD Publishing. http://
    dx.doi.org/10.1787/eco_surveys-can-2012-en (March 2015)

4   Domestic Spending on Research and Development, Statistics Canada, Fall
    2014

5   Conference Board of Canada website: http://www.conferenceboard.ca/hcp/
    details/innovation.aspx

6   OECD (2014), *OECD Factbook 2014: Economic, Environmental and Social*

Statistics, OECD Publishing. http://dx.doi.org/10.1787/factbook-2014-en (March 2015); p 157

7 OECD (2012), *OECD Economic Surveys: Canada 2012*, OECD Publishing. http://dx.doi.org/10.1787/eco_surveys-can-2012-en (March 2015), p. 29

8 Crane, David, "Crane: Canadians can't afford to lose productivity race," *Toronto Star*, March 31, 2010

9 Stanford, Jim, "Corporate Canada's enemy lurks within," *Globe and Mail*, June 5, 2009

10 Parkinson, David, "Canada slips a notch in competitiveness ranking," *Globe and Mail*, September 3, 2014

11 Berthiaume, Lee, "With the F-35 price tag on the rise, Canada will be faced with ponying up an extra $1B or cut back purchase," *Postmedia News*, December 10, 2014

CHAPTER 9

1 Stanford, Jim, "That strong recovery? It was just a myth," *Globe and Mail*, August 11, 2014

2 Campion-Smith, Bruce, "Ottawa faces deficit with low oil prices, budget watchdog says," *Toronto Star*, January 26, 2015

3 Ibid.

4 Hepburn, Andrew, "What Canada's current account deficit says about our vulnerability to a global slowdown," *Maclean's Magazine*, September 13, 2012

5 OECD (2014), *OECD Factbook 2014: Economic, Environmental and Social Statistics*, OECD Publishing. http://dx.doi.org/10.1787/factbook-2014-en (March 2015), p. 77

6 Statistics Canada, *National Accounts*, Canada's Cumulative Trade Balance, 2014

7 Gross General Government Debt % of GDP, 2013, IMF Fiscal Monitor, Federal and Provincial Budgets, CFIB Economics Estimates

8 "Canadian Economic Growth Slides With Decline in Oil," Conference Board of Canada, February 9, 2015

9 OECD (2014), *OECD Factbook 2014: Economic, Environmental and Social Statistics*, OECD Publishing. http://dx.doi.org/10.1787/factbook-2014-en (March 2015), p. 35

10 Ibid., p. 41

11 Ibid., p. 133, 137

12 Ibid., p. 143

13 Ibid., p. 145

14 "CLC Analysis of the 2013 Federal Budget," Canadian Labour Congress, March 21, 2013

15 Grant, Tavia, "Canada jobless rate ticks up as labour participation stuck in 13 year low," *Globe and Mail*, December 5, 2014

16 OECD (2014), OECD *Factbook 2014: Economic, Environmental and Social Statistics*, OECD Publishing. http://dx.doi.org/10.1787/factbook-2014-en (March 2015), p. 49

17 Ibid. p. 163

18 Ibid., p. 185

19 Ibid., p. 155

20 Ibid., p. 195

21 Ibid., p. 217

22 Ibid., p. 249, 253

23 Ibid., p. 239

24 Ibid., p. 231

25 Stanford, Jim, "Canada's sluggish labour market and the myth of the skills shortage," *Academic Matters*, November 2013

26 Stanford, Jim, "Canada's Incomplete, Mediocre Recovery," *Alternative Federal Budget 2012, Technical Paper*, Canadian Centre for Policy Alternatives, January 2012

27 Ibid.

28 Goodale, Ralph, "Harper's Growth Record Is the Worst Since R.B. Bennett," *Huffington Post*, September 6, 2013

29 Ibid.

30 Goodale, Ralph, "Mr. Harper's 9 Years Have Weakened Our Economy," Blogpost, March 9, 2015

31 Department of Finance Fiscal Reference Tables, Government of Canada, 2014

32 May, Kathryn, "Federal government on track to cut 35,000 public service jobs," *Ottawa Citizen*, August 27, 2014

33 Public Accounts of Canada, 2013–2014, Volume 1, Summary Report and Consolidated Financial Statements, Receiver General for Canada (for the year ending March 31, 2014), October 28, 2014

34 Department of Finance Fiscal Reference Tables, Government of Canada, 2014

35 Public Accounts of Canada, 2013–2014, Volume 1, Summary Report and Consolidated Financial Statements, Receiver General for Canada (for the year ending March 31, 2014), October 28, 2014

36 Freeman, Sunny, "NAFTA's Chapter 11 Makes Canada Most-Sued Country Under Free Trade Tribunals," *Huffington Post*, January 14, 2015

37 Foreign Affairs, Trade and Development Canada website: Canada's Free Trade Agreements, 2015

38 Letter from Maude Barlow, Council of Canadians Newsletter, September 12, 2014

CHAPTER 10

1   *Globe and Mail*, April 14, 2007
2   *Society at a Glance*, 2006, OECD.
3   *Globe and Mail*, October 20, 2007.
4   To be exact, 174,661 people made donations out of a total of 23,054,614 eligible voters, for a percentage of 0.76.
5   Fair Vote Canada, October, 2014
6   Goar, Carol, "Election Financing Comes Clean," *Toronto Star*, January 3, 2007
7   A fuller description of the workings of an MMP system can be found on Fair Vote Canada's website: www.fairvotecanada.org. The Law Commission of Canada's report is titled Voting Counts: Electoral Reform in Canada and is available online through the Government of Canada website.
8   An excellent source of comparative international data appears in Arend Lijphart, Patterns of Democracy, Government Forms and Performance in Thirty-Six Countries (New Haven: Yale University Press, 1999). Fair Vote Canada also has a 10-page summary of key findings: "Can Fair Voting Systems Really Make a Difference?" available on its website.
9   McGregor, Roy, "Ontario referendum flying under the radar—even with Air Farce." *Globe and Mail*, October 1, 2007
10   CCPA Monitor, September, 2004.

MEL HURTIG is the legendary Edmonton bookseller, publisher and creator of *The Canadian Encyclopedia* who became a political activist, then an author in 1991 with his huge bestseller *The Betrayal of Canada*. He is also the author of *Pay the Rent or Feed the Kids, The Vanishing Country, Rushing to Armageddon* and *The Truth About Canada*. He is an Officer of the Order of Canada, and has received many honorary degrees and other honours. He lives in Vancouver.

CPSIA information can be obtained at www.ICGtesting.com
Printed in the USA
LVOW07s2110160615

442685LV00001B/1/P